A PLUME BOOK

FENCES

AUGUST WILSON is one of America's leading playwrights, whose work has been acclaimed as among the finest of the American theater. His first play, *Ma Rainey's Black Bottom*, won the New York Drama Critics' Circle Award for best new play. His second play, *Fences*, won numerous awards, including the Tony Award, the New York Drama Critics' Circle Award, the Drama Desk Award, and the Pulitzer Prize. His third play, *Joe Turner's Come and Gone*, also was best play of the year by the New York Drama Critics' Circle. *The Piano Lesson* (1990) won the Pulitzer Prize for Drama. August Wilson passed away in 2005.

LLOYD RICHARDS was dean of Yale School of Drama and artistic director of Yale Repertory Theatre. He died in 2006.

Praise for *Fences*

"What makes *Fences* so engrossing, so embracing, so simply powerful, is Wilson's startling ability to tell a story, reveal feeling, paint emotion."
—Clive Barnes, *New York Post*

"*Fences* is an eloquent play . . . a comedy-drama that is well-nigh flawless. . . . Life, in all its bittersweetness, fills the stage . . . pain and anger are balanced by humor and common sense, and both passion and compassion are played on a muted trumpet that insinuates rather than insists. *Fences* marks a long step forward for Wilson's dramaturgy."
—John Simon, *New York Magazine*

"A moving story line and a hero almost Shakespearian in contour."
—Sylviane Gold, *The Wall Street Journal*

"A work of tremendous impact that summons up gratitude for the beauty of its language, the truth of its character, the power of its portrayals."
—*Chicago Tribune*

FENCES

A PLAY BY
AUGUST WILSON

Introduction by Lloyd Richards

PLUME

PLUME
An imprint of Penguin Random House LLC
375 Hudson Street
New York, New York 10014

First Plume printing, June 1986

P REGISTERED TRADEMARK—MARCA REGISTRADA

LIBRARY OF CONGRESS CATALOGING-IN-PUBLICATION DATA
Wilson, August.
Fences : a play in two acts.

I. Title.
PS3573.I45677F4   1986   812'54   86-5264
ISBN 978-0-452-26401-4
Plume movie tie-in edition ISBN: 9780735216686

Printed in the United States of America
1   3   5   7   9   10   8   6   4   2

for Lloyd Richards,
who adds to whatever he touches

Fences is the second major play of a poet turned playwright, August Wilson. One of the most compelling storytellers to begin writing for the theater in many years, he has taken the responsibility of telling the tale of the encounter of the released black slaves with a vigorous and ruthless growing America decade by decade. *Fences* encompasses the 1950s and a black family trying to put down roots in the slag slippery hills of a middle American urban industrial city that one might correctly mistake for Pittsburgh, Pennsylvania.

To call August Wilson a storyteller is to align him at one and the same time with the ancient aristocrats of dramatic writing who stood before the tribes and made compelling oral history into legend, as well as with the modern playwrights who bring an audience to their feet at the end of an evening of their work because that audience knows that they have encountered themselves, their concerns, and their passions, and have been moved and enriched by the experience. In *Fences,* August Wilson tells the story of four generations of black Americans and of how they have passed on a legacy of morals, mores, attitudes, and patterns through stories with and without music.

He tells the story of Troy Maxson, born to a sharecropper father who was frustrated by the fact that every crop took him further into debt. The father knew himself as a failure and took it out on everyone at hand, including his young son, Troy, and his wives, all of whom "leave him." Troy learns violence from him, but he also learns the value of work and the fact that a man takes responsibility for his family no matter how difficult circumstances may be. He learns respect for a home, the importance of owning land, and the value of an education because he doesn't have one.

An excellent baseball player, Troy learns that in the land of equal opportunity, chances for a black man are not always equal, and that the same country that deprived him asked sacrifice of his brother in World War II and got it. Half his brother's head was blown away, and he is now a disoriented and confused beautiful man. He learns that he must fight and win the little victories that—given his life—must assume the proportion of major triumphs. He learns that day to day and moment to moment he lives close to death and must wrestle with death to survive. He learns that to take a chance and grab a moment of beauty can crumble the delicate fabric of an intricate value system and leave one desolate and alone. Strength of body and strength of purpose are not enough. Chance and the color of one's skin, chance again, can tip the balance. "You've got to take the crooked with the straight."

Troy Maxson spins yarns, raps, tells stories to his family and friends in that wonderful environment of the pretelevision, pre-airconditioned era when the back porch and the backyard were the platform for some of the most exciting tales of that time. From this platform and through his behavior he passes on to his extended family principles for living, which members of his family accept or refute through the manner in which they choose to live their own lives.

How is this reformed criminal perceived? What should be learned from him? What accepted? What passed on? Is his life to be discarded or honored? That is the story of *Fences*, which we build to keep things and people out or in.

New Haven, Connecticut
March 6, 1986

FENCES

When the sins of our fathers visit us
We do not have to play host.
We can banish them with forgiveness
As God, in His Largeness and Laws.
                                    —August Wilson

Fences opened on April 30, 1985, at the Yale Repertory Theatre in New Haven, Connecticut, with the following cast:

TROY MAXSON	*James Earl Jones*
JIM BONO	*Ray Aranha*
ROSE	*Mary Alice*
LYONS	*Charles Brown*
GABRIEL	*Russell Costen*
CORY	*Courtney B. Vance*
RAYNELL	*Cristal Coleman* and *LaJara Henderson* at alternate performances

Director: Lloyd Richards
Set Design: James D. Sandefur
Costume Design: Candice Donnelly
Light Design: Danianne Mizzy
Music Director: Dwight Andrews
Production Stage Manager: Joel Grynheim
Stage Manager: Terrence J. Witter
Casting: Meg Simon/Fran Kumin

Fences was initially presented as a staged reading at the Eugene O'Neill Theater Center's 1983 National Playwrights Conference.

Fences opened on March 26, 1987, at the 46th Street Theatre, with the following cast:

TROY MAXSON	*James Earl Jones*
JIM BONO	*Ray Aranha*
ROSE	*Mary Alice*
LYONS	*Charles Brown*
GABRIEL	*Frankie R. Faison*
CORY	*Courtney B. Vance*
RAYNELL	*Karima Miller*

Producer: Carole Shorenstein Hays in association with The Yale Repertory Theatre
Director: Lloyd Richards
Set Design: James D. Sandefur
Costume Design: Candice Donnelly
Light Design: Danianne Mizzy
Music Director: Dwight Andrews
Production Stage Manager: Martin Gold
General Manager: Robert Kamlot
Stage Manager: Terrence J. Witter
Casting: Meg Simon/Fran Kumin

Fences was initially presented as a staged reading at the Eugene O'Neill Theater Center's 1983 National Playwrights Conference.

This new edition, first printed in May 1987, reflects the final definintive text of FENCES as performed on Broadway.

Characters

TROY MAXSON
JIM BONO   TROY's *friend*
ROSE   TROY's *wife*
LYONS   TROY's *oldest son by previous marriage*
GABRIEL   TROY's *brother*
CORY   TROY *and* ROSE's *son*
RAYNELL   TROY's *daughter*

The setting is the yard which fronts the only entrance to the MAXSON household, an ancient two-story brick house set back off a small alley in a big-city neighborhood. The entrance to the house is gained by two or three steps leading to a wooden porch badly in need of paint.

A relatively recent addition to the house and running its full width, the porch lacks congruence. It is a sturdy porch with a flat roof. One or two chairs of dubious value sit at one end where the kitchen window opens onto the porch. An old-fashioned icebox stands silent guard at the opposite end.

The yard is a small dirt yard, partially fenced, except for the last scene, with a wooden sawhorse, a pile of lumber, and other fence-building equipment set off to the side. Opposite is a tree from which hangs a ball made of rags. A baseball bat leans against the tree. Two oil drums serve as garbage receptacles and sit near the house at right to complete the setting.

The Play

Near the turn of the century, the destitute of Europe sprang on the city with tenacious claws and an honest and solid dream. The city devoured them. They swelled its belly until it burst into a thousand furnaces and sewing machines, a thousand butcher shops and bakers' ovens, a thousand churches and hospitals and funeral parlors and money-lenders. The city grew. It nourished itself and offered each man a partnership limited only by his talent, his guile, and his willingness and capacity for hard work. For the immigrants of Europe, a dream dared and won true.

The descendants of African slaves were offered no such welcome or participation. They came from places called the Carolinas and the Virginias, Georgia, Alabama, Mississippi, and Tennessee. They came strong, eager, searching. The city rejected them and they fled and settled along the riverbanks and under bridges in shallow, ramshackle houses made of sticks and tar-paper. They collected rags and wood. They sold the use of their muscles and their bodies. They cleaned houses and washed clothes, they shined shoes, and in quiet desperation and vengeful pride, they stole, and lived in pursuit of their own dream. That they could breathe free, finally, and stand to meet life with the force of dignity and whatever eloquence the heart could call upon.

By 1957, the hard-won victories of the European immigrants had solidified the industrial might of America. War had been confronted and won with new energies that used loyalty and patriotism as its fuel. Life was rich, full, and flourishing. The Milwaukee Braves won the World Series, and the hot winds of change that would make the sixties a turbulent, racing, dangerous, and provocative decade had not yet begun to blow full.

Act One

It is 1957. TROY *and* BONO *enter the yard, engaged in conversation.* TROY *is fifty-three years old, a large man with thick, heavy hands; it is this largeness that he strives to fill out and make an accommodation with. Together with his blackness, his largeness informs his sensibilities and the choices he has made in his life.*

Of the two men, BONO *is obviously the follower. His commitment to their friendship of thirty-odd years is rooted in his admiration of* TROY'*s honesty, capacity for hard work, and his strength, which* BONO *seeks to emulate.*

It is Friday night, payday, and the one night of the week the two men engage in a ritual of talk and drink. TROY *is usually the most talkative and at times he can be crude and almost vulgar, though he is capable of rising to profound heights of expression. The men carry lunch buckets and wear or carry burlap aprons and are dressed in clothes suitable to their jobs as garbage collectors.*

BONO: Troy, you ought to stop that lying!

TROY: I ain't lying! The nigger had a watermelon this big.
(*He indicates with his hands.*)

Talking about . . . "What watermelon, Mr. Rand?" I liked to fell out! "What watermelon, Mr. Rand?" . . . And it sitting there big as life.

BONO: What did Mr. Rand say?

TROY: Ain't said nothing. Figure if the nigger too dumb to know he carrying a watermelon, he wasn't gonna get much sense out of him. Trying to hide that great big old watermelon under his coat. Afraid to let the white man see him carry it home.

BONO: I'm like you . . . I ain't got no time for them kind of people.

TROY: Now what he look like getting mad cause he see the man from the union talking to Mr. Rand?

BONO: He come to me talking about . . . "Maxson gonna get us fired." I told him to get away from me with that. He walked away from me calling you a troublemaker. What Mr. Rand say?

TROY: Ain't said nothing. He told me to go down the Commissioner's office next Friday. They called me down there to see them.

BONO: Well, as long as you got your complaint filed, they can't fire you. That's what one of them white fellows tell me.

TROY: I ain't worried about them firing me. They gonna fire me cause I asked a question? That's all I did. I went to Mr. Rand and asked him, "Why?" Why you got the white mens driving and the colored lifting?" Told him, "what's the matter, don't I count? You think only white fellows got sense enough to drive a truck. That ain't no paper job! Hell, anybody can drive a truck. How come you got all whites driving and the colored lifting? He told me "take it to the union." Well, hell, that's what I done! Now they wanna come up with this pack of lies.

BONO: I told Brownie if the man come and ask him any questions . . . just tell the truth! It ain't nothing but something they done trumped up on you cause you filed a complaint on them.

TROY: Brownie don't understand nothing. All I want them to do is change the job description. Give everybody a chance to drive the truck. Brownie can't see that. He ain't got that much sense.

BONO: How you figure he be making out with that gal be up at Taylors' all the time . . . that Alberta gal?

TROY: Same as you and me. Getting just as much as we is. Which is to say nothing.

BONO: It is, huh? I figure you doing a little better than me . . . and I ain't saying what I'm doing.

TROY: Aw, nigger, look here . . . I know you. If you had got anywhere near that gal, twenty minutes later you be looking to tell somebody. And the first one you gonna tell . . . that you gonna want to brag to . . . is gonna be me.

BONO: I ain't saying that. I see where you be eyeing her.

TROY: I eye all the women. I don't miss nothing. Don't never let nobody tell you Troy Maxson don't eye the women.

BONO: You been doing more than eyeing her. You done bought her a drink or two.

TROY: Hell yeah, I bought her a drink! What that mean? I bought you one, too. What that mean cause I buy her a drink? I'm just being polite.

BONO: It's alright to buy her one drink. That's what you call being polite. But when you wanna be buying two or three . . . that's what you call eyeing her.

TROY: Look here, as long as you known me . . . you ever known me to chase after women?

BONO: Hell yeah! Long as I done known you. You forgetting I knew you when.

TROY: Naw, I'm talking about since I been married to Rose?

BONO: Oh, not since you been married to Rose. Now, that's the truth, there. I can say that.

TROY: Alright then! Case closed.

BONO: I see you be walking up around Alberta's house. You supposed to be at Taylors' and you be walking up around there.

TROY: What you watching where I'm walking for? I ain't watching after you.

BONO: I seen you walking around there more than once.

TROY: Hell, you liable to see me walking anywhere! That don't mean nothing cause you see me walking around there.

BONO: Where she come from anyway? She just kinda showed up one day.

TROY: Tallahassee. You can look at her and tell she one of them Florida gals. They got some big healthy women down there. Grow them right up out the ground. Got a little bit of Indian in her. Most of them niggers down in Florida got some Indian in them.

BONO: I don't know about that Indian part. But she damn

sure big and healthy. Woman wear some big stockings. Got them great big old legs and hips as wide as the Mississippi River.

TROY: Legs don't mean nothing. You don't do nothing but push them out of the way. But them hips cushion the ride!

BONO: Troy, you ain't got no sense.

TROY: It's the truth! Like you riding on Goodyears!
(ROSE *enters from the house. She is ten years younger than* TROY, *her devotion to him stems from her recognition of the possibilities of her life without him: a succession of abusive men and their babies, a life of partying and running the streets, the Church, or aloneness with its attendant pain and frustration. She recognizes* TROY's *spirit as a fine and illuminating one and she either ignores or forgives his faults, only some of which she recognizes. Though she doesn't drink, her presence is an integral part of the Friday night rituals. She alternates between the porch and the kitchen, where supper preparations are under way.*)

ROSE: What you all out here getting into?

TROY: What you worried about what we getting into for? This is men talk, woman.

ROSE: What I care what you all talking about? Bono, you gonna stay for supper?

BONO: No, I thank you, Rose. But Lucille say she cooking up a pot of pigfeet.

TROY: Pigfeet! Hell, I'm going home with you! Might even stay the night if you got some pigfeet. You got something in there to top them pigfeet, Rose?

ROSE: I'm cooking up some chicken. I got some chicken and collard greens.

TROY: Well, go on back in the house and let me and Bono finish what we was talking about. This is men talk. I got some talk for you later. You know what kind of talk I mean. You go on and powder it up.

ROSE: Troy Maxson, don't you start that now!

TROY: (*Puts his arm around her.*) Aw, woman . . . come here. Look here, Bono . . . when I met this woman . . . I got out that place, say, "Hitch up my pony, saddle up my mare . . . there's a woman out there for me somewhere. I looked here. Looked there. Saw Rose and latched on to her." I latched on to her and told her—I'm gonna tell you the truth—I told her, "Baby, I don't wanna marry, I just wanna be your man." Rose told me . . . tell him what you told me, Rose.

ROSE: I told him if he wasn't the marrying kind, then move out the way so the marrying kind could find me.

TROY: That's what she told me. "Nigger, you in my way. You blocking the view! Move out the way so I can find me a husband." I thought it over two or three days. Come back—

ROSE: Ain't no two or three days nothing. You was back the same night.

TROY: Come back, told her . . . "Okay, baby . . . but I'm gonna buy me a banty rooster and put him out there in the backyard . . . and when he see a stranger come, he'll flap his wings and crow . . ." Look here, Bono, I could watch the front door by myself . . . it was that back door I was worried about.

ROSE: Troy, you ought not talk like that. Troy ain't doing nothing but telling a lie.

TROY: Only thing is . . . when we first got married . . . forget the rooster . . . we ain't had no yard!

BONO: I hear you tell it. Me and Lucille was staying down there on Logan Street. Had two rooms with the outhouse in the back. I ain't mind the outhouse none. But when that goddamn wind blow through there in the winter . . . that's what I'm talking about! To this day I wonder why in the hell I ever stayed down there for six long years. But see, I didn't know I could do no better. I thought only white folks had inside toilets and things.

ROSE: There's a lot of people don't know they can do no better than they doing now. That's just something you got to learn. A lot of folks still shop at Bella's.

TROY: Ain't nothing wrong with shopping at Bella's. She got fresh food.

ROSE: I ain't said nothing about if she got fresh food. I'm talking about what she charge. She charge ten cents more than the A&P.

TROY: The A&P ain't never done nothing for me. I spends my money where I'm treated right. I go down to Bella, say, "I need a loaf of bread, I'll pay you Friday." She give it to me. What sense that make when I got money to go and spend it somewhere else and ignore the person who done right by me? That ain't in the Bible.

ROSE: We ain't talking about what's in the Bible. What sense it make to shop there when she overcharge?

TROY: You shop where you want to. I'll do my shopping where the people been good to me.

ROSE: Well, I don't think it's right for her to overcharge. That's all I was saying.

BONO: Look here . . . I got to get on. Lucille going be raising all kind of hell.

TROY: Where you going, nigger? We ain't finished this pint. Come here, finish this pint.

BONO: Well, hell, I am . . . if you ever turn the bottle loose.

TROY: (*Hands him the bottle.*) The only thing I say about the A&P is I'm glad Cory got that job down there. Help him take care of his school clothes and things. Gabe done moved out and things getting tight around here. He got that job. . . . He can start to look out for himself.

ROSE: Cory done went and got recruited by a college football team.

TROY: I told that boy about that football stuff. The white man ain't gonna let him get nowhere with that football. I told him when he first come to me with it. Now you come telling me he done went and got more tied up in it. He ought to go and get recruited in how to fix cars or something where he can make a living.

ROSE: He ain't talking about making no living playing football. It's just something the boys in school do. They gonna send a recruiter by to talk to you. He'll tell you he ain't talking about making no living playing football. It's a honor to be recruited.

TROY: It ain't gonna get him nowhere. Bono'll tell you that.

BONO: If he be like you in the sports . . . he's gonna be

alright. Ain't but two men ever played baseball as good as you. That's Babe Ruth and Josh Gibson. Them's the only two men ever hit more home runs than you.

TROY: What it ever get me? Ain't got a pot to piss in or a window to throw it out of.

ROSE: Times have changed since you was playing baseball, Troy. That was before the war. Times have changed a lot since then.

TROY: How in hell they done changed?

ROSE: They got lots of colored boys playing ball now. Baseball and football.

BONO: You right about that, Rose. Times have changed, Troy. You just come along too early.

TROY: There ought not never have been no time called too early! Now you take that fellow . . . what's that fellow they had playing right field for the Yankees back then? You know who I'm talking about, Bono. Used to play right field for the Yankees.

ROSE: Selkirk?

TROY: Selkirk! That's it! Man batting .269, understand? .269. What kind of sense that make? I was hitting .432 with thirty-seven home runs! Man batting .269 and playing right field for the Yankees! I saw Josh Gibson's daughter yesterday. She walking around with raggedy shoes on her feet. Now I bet you Selkirk's daughter ain't walking around with raggedy shoes on her feet! I bet you that!

ROSE: They got a lot of colored baseball players now. Jackie Robinson was the first. Folks had to wait for Jackie Robinson.

TROY: I done seen a hundred niggers play baseball better than Jackie Robinson. Hell, I know some teams Jackie Robinson couldn't even make! What you talking about Jackie Robinson. Jackie Robinson wasn't nobody. I'm talking about if you could play ball then they ought to have let you play. Don't care what color you were. Come telling me I come along too early. If you could play . . . then they ought to have let you play.
(TROY *takes a long drink from the bottle.*)

ROSE: You gonna drink yourself to death. You don't need to be drinking like that.

TROY: Death ain't nothing. I done seen him. Done wrassled with him. You can't tell me nothing about death. Death ain't nothing but a fastball on the outside corner. And you know what I'll do to that! Lookee here, Bono . . . am I lying? You get one of them fastballs, about waist high, over the outside corner of the plate where you can get the meat of the bat on it . . . and good god! You can kiss it goodbye. Now, am I lying?

BONO: Naw, you telling the truth there. I seen you do it.

TROY: If I'm lying . . . that 450 feet worth of lying!
(*Pause.*)
That's all death is to me. A fastball on the outside corner.

ROSE: I don't know why you want to get on talking about death.

TROY: Ain't nothing wrong with talking about death. That's part of life. Everybody gonna die. You gonna die, I'm gonna die. Bono's gonna die. Hell, we all gonna die.

ROSE: But you ain't got to talk about it. I don't like to talk about it.

TROY: You the one brought it up. Me and Bono was talking about baseball . . . you tell me I'm gonna drink myself to death. Ain't that right, Bono? You know I don't drink this but one night out of the week. That's Friday night. I'm gonna drink just enough to where I can handle it. Then I cuts it loose. I leave it alone. So don't you worry about me drinking myself to death. 'Cause I ain't worried about Death. I done seen him. I done wrestled with him.

Look here, Bono . . . I looked up one day and Death was marching straight at me. Like Soldiers on Parade! The Army of Death was marching straight at me. The middle of July, 1941. It got real cold just like it be winter. It seem like Death himself reached out and touched me on the shoulder. He touch me just like I touch you. I got cold as ice and Death standing there grinning at me.

ROSE: Troy, why don't you hush that talk.

TROY: I say . . . What you want, Mr. Death? You be wanting me? You done brought your army to be getting me? I looked him dead in the eye. I wasn't fearing nothing. I was ready to tangle. Just like I'm ready to tangle now. The Bible say be ever vigilant. That's why I don't get but so drunk. I got to keep watch.

ROSE: Troy was right down there in Mercy Hospital. You remember he had pneumonia? Laying there with a fever talking plumb out of his head.

TROY: Death standing there staring at me . . . carrying that sickle in his hand. Finally he say, "You want bound over for another year?" See, just like that . . . "You want bound over for another year?" I told him, "Bound over hell! Let's settle this now!"

It seem like he kinda fell back when I said that, and all the cold went out of me. I reached down and grabbed that sickle and threw it just as far as I could throw it . . . and me and him commenced to wrestling.

We wrestled for three days and three nights. I can't say where I found the strength from. Every time it seemed like he was gonna get the best of me, I'd reach way down deep inside myself and find the strength to do him one better.

ROSE: Every time Troy tell that story he find different ways to tell it. Different things to make up about it.

TROY: I ain't making up nothing. I'm telling you the facts of what happened. I wrestled with Death for three days and three nights and I'm standing here to tell you about it.

(*Pause.*)

Alright. At the end of the third night we done weakened each other to where we can't hardly move. Death stood up, throwed on his robe . . . had him a white robe with a hood on it. He throwed on that robe and went off to look for his sickle. Say, "I'll be back." Just like that. "I'll be back." I told him, say, "Yeah, but . . . you gonna have to find me!" I wasn't no fool. I wasn't going looking for him. Death ain't nothing to play with. And I know he's gonna get me. I know I got to join his army . . . his camp followers. But as long as I keep my strength and see him coming . . . as long as I keep up my vigilance . . . he's gonna have to fight to get me. I ain't going easy.

BONO: Well, look here, since you got to keep up your vigilance . . . let me have the bottle.

TROY: Aw hell, I shouldn't have told you that part. I should have left out that part.

ROSE: Troy be talking that stuff and half the time don't even know what he be talking about.

TROY: Bono know me better than that.

BONO: That's right. I know you. I know you got some Uncle Remus in your blood. You got more stories than the devil got sinners.

TROY: Aw hell, I done seen him too! Done talked with the devil.

ROSE: Troy, don't nobody wanna be hearing all that stuff. (*LYONS enters the yard from the street. Thirty-four years old, TROY's son by a previous marriage, he sports a neatly trimmed goatee, sport coat, white shirt, tieless and buttoned at the collar. Though he fancies himself a musician, he is more caught up in the rituals and "idea" of being a musician than in the actual practice of the music. He has come to borrow money from TROY, and while he knows he will be successful, he is uncertain as to what extent his lifestyle will be held up to scrutiny and ridicule.*)

LYONS: Hey, Pop.

TROY: What you come "Hey, Popping" me for?

LYONS: How you doing, Rose?
(*He kisses her.*)
Mr. Bono. How you doing?

BONO: Hey, Lyons . . . how you been?

TROY: He must have been doing alright. I ain't seen him around here last week.

ROSE: Troy, leave your boy alone. He come by to see you and you wanna start all that nonsense.

TROY: I ain't bothering Lyons.
(*Offers him the bottle.*)
Here . . . get you a drink. We got an understanding. I know why he come by to see me and he know I know.

LYONS: Come on, Pop . . . I just stopped by to say hi . . . see how you was doing.

TROY: You ain't stopped by yesterday.

ROSE: You gonna stay for supper, Lyons? I got some chicken cooking in the oven.

LYONS: No, Rose . . . thanks. I was just in the neighborhood and thought I'd stop by for a minute.

TROY: You was in the neighborhood alright, nigger. You telling the truth there. You was in the neighborhood cause it's my payday.

LYONS: Well, hell, since you mentioned it . . . let me have ten dollars.

TROY: I'll be damned! I'll die and go to hell and play blackjack with the devil before I give you ten dollars.

BONO: That's what I wanna know about . . . that devil you done seen.

LYONS: What . . . Pop done seen the devil? You too much, Pops.

TROY: Yeah, I done seen him. Talked to him too!

ROSE: You ain't seen no devil. I done told you that man ain't had nothing to do with the devil. Anything you can't understand, you want to call it the devil.

TROY: Look here, Bono . . . I went down to see Hertz-berger about some furniture. Got three rooms for two-ninety-eight. That what it say on the radio. "Three rooms . . . two-ninety-eight." Even made up a little song about it. Go down there . . . man tell me I can't get no credit. I'm working every day and can't get no credit. What to do? I got an empty house with some raggedy furniture in it. Cory ain't got no bed. He's sleeping on a pile of rags on the floor. Working every day and can't get no credit. Come back here—Rose'll tell you—madder than hell. Sit down . . . try to figure what I'm gonna do. Come a knock on the door. Ain't been living here but three days. Who know I'm here? Open the door . . . devil standing there bigger than life. White fellow . . . got on good clothes and everything. Standing there with a clipboard in his hand. I ain't had to say nothing. First words come out of his mouth was . . . "I understand you need some furniture and can't get no credit." I liked to fell over. He say "I'll give you all the credit you want, but you got to pay the interest on it." I told him, "Give me three rooms worth and charge whatever you want." Next day a truck pulled up here and two men unloaded them three rooms. Man what drove the truck give me a book. Say send ten dollars, first of every month to the address in the book and everything will be alright. Say if I miss a payment the devil was coming back and it'll be hell to pay. That was fifteen years ago. To this day . . . the first of the month I send my ten dollars, Rose'll tell you.

ROSE: Troy lying.

TROY: I ain't never seen that man since. Now you tell me who else that could have been but the devil? I ain't sold my soul or nothing like that, you understand. Naw, I wouldn't have truck with the devil about nothing like that. I got my furniture and pays my ten dollars the first of the month just like clockwork.

BONO: How long you say you been paying this ten dollars a month?

TROY: Fifteen years!

BONO: Hell, ain't you finished paying for it yet? How much the man done charged you.

TROY: Aw hell, I done paid for it. I done paid for it ten times over! The fact is I'm scared to stop paying it.

ROSE: Troy lying. We got that furniture from Mr. Glickman. He ain't paying no ten dollars a month to nobody.

TROY: Aw hell, woman. Bono know I ain't that big a fool.

LYONS: I was just getting ready to say . . . I know where there's a bridge for sale.

TROY: Look here, I'll tell you this . . . it don't matter to me if he was the devil. It don't matter if the devil give credit. Somebody has got to give it.

ROSE: It ought to matter. You going around talking about having truck with the devil . . . God's the one you gonna have to answer to. He's the one gonna be at the Judgment.

LYONS: Yeah, well, look here, Pop . . . let me have that ten dollars. I'll give it back to you. Bonnie got a job working at the hospital.

TROY: What I tell you, Bono? The only time I see this nigger is when he wants something. That's the only time I see him.

LYONS: Come on, Pop, Mr. Bono don't want to hear all that. Let me have the ten dollars. I told you Bonnie working.

TROY: What that mean to me? "Bonnie working." I don't care if she working. Go ask her for the ten dollars if she working. Talking about "Bonnie working." Why ain't you working?

LYONS: Aw, Pop, you know I can't find no decent job. Where am I gonna get a job at? You know I can't get no job.

TROY: I told you I know some people down there. I can get you on the rubbish if you want to work. I told you that the last time you came by here asking me for something.

LYONS: Naw, Pop . . . thanks. That ain't for me. I don't wanna be carrying nobody's rubbish. I don't wanna be punching nobody's time clock.

TROY: What's the matter, you too good to carry people's rubbish? Where you think that ten dollars you talking about come from? I'm just supposed to haul people's rubbish and give my money to you cause you too lazy to work. You too lazy to work and wanna know why you ain't got what I got.

ROSE: What hospital Bonnie working at? Mercy?

LYONS: She's down at Passavant working in the laundry.

TROY: I ain't got nothing as it is. I give you that ten dollars and I got to eat beans the rest of the week. Naw . . . you ain't getting no ten dollars here.

LYONS: You ain't got to be eating no beans. I don't know why you wanna say that.

TROY: I ain't got no extra money. Gabe done moved over to Miss Pearl's paying her the rent and things done got tight around here. I can't afford to be giving you every payday.

LYONS: I ain't asked you to give me nothing. I asked you to loan me ten dollars. I know you got ten dollars.

TROY: Yeah, I got it. You know why I got it? Cause I don't throw my money away out there in the streets. You living the fast life . . . wanna be a musician . . . running around in them clubs and things . . . then, you learn to take care of yourself. You ain't gonna find me going and asking nobody for nothing. I done spent too many years without.

LYONS: You and me is two different people, Pop.

TROY: I done learned my mistake and learned to do what's right by it. You still trying to get something for nothing. Life don't owe you nothing. You owe it to yourself. Ask Bono. He'll tell you I'm right.

LYONS: You got your way of dealing with the world . . . I got mine. The only thing that matters to me is the music.

TROY: Yeah, I can see that! It don't matter how you gonna eat . . . where your next dollar is coming from. You telling the truth there.

LYONS: I know I got to eat. But I got to live too. I need something that gonna help me to get out of the bed in the morning. Make me feel like I belong in the world. I don't bother nobody. I just stay with my music cause that's the only way I can find to live in the world. Otherwise there ain't no telling what I might do. Now I don't come criticizing you and how you live. I just come by to ask you for ten dollars. I don't wanna hear all that about how I live.

TROY: Boy, your mama did a hell of a job raising you.

LYONS: You can't change me, Pop. I'm thirty-four years old. If you wanted to change me, you should have been there when I was growing up. I come by to see you . . .

ask for ten dollars and you want to talk about how I was raised. You don't know nothing about how I was raised.

ROSE: Let the boy have ten dollars, Troy.

TROY: (*To LYONS.*) What the hell you looking at me for? I ain't got no ten dollars. You know what I do with my money.
(*To ROSE.*)
Give him ten dollars if you want him to have it.

ROSE: I will. Just as soon as you turn it loose.

TROY: (*Handing ROSE the money.*) There it is. Seventy-six dollars and forty-two cents. You see this, Bono? Now, I ain't gonna get but six of that back.

ROSE: You ought to stop telling that lie. Here, Lyons.
(*She hands him the money.*)

LYONS: Thanks, Rose. Look . . . I got to run . . . I'll see you later.

TROY: Wait a minute. You gonna say, "thanks, Rose" and ain't gonna look to see where she got that ten dollars from? See how they do me, Bono?

LYONS: I know she got it from you, Pop. Thanks. I'll give it back to you.

TROY: There he go telling another lie. Time I see that ten dollars . . . he'll be owing me thirty more.

LYONS: See you, Mr. Bono.

BONO: Take care, Lyons!

LYONS: Thanks, Pop. I'll see you again.
(*LYONS exits the yard.*)

TROY: I don't know why he don't go and get him a decent job and take care of that woman he got.

BONO: He'll be alright, Troy. The boy is still young.

TROY: The *boy* is thirty-four years old.

ROSE: Let's not get off into all that.

BONO: Look here . . . I got to be going. I got to be getting on. Lucille gonna be waiting.

TROY: (*Puts his arm around* ROSE.) See this woman, Bono? I love this woman. I love this woman so much it hurts. I love her so much . . . I done run out of ways of loving her. So I got to go back to basics. Don't you come by my house Monday morning talking about time to go to work . . . 'cause I'm still gonna be stroking!

ROSE: Troy! Stop it now!

BONO: I ain't paying him no mind, Rose. That ain't nothing but gin-talk. Go on, Troy. I'll see you Monday.

TROY: Don't you come by my house, nigger! I done told you what I'm gonna be doing.
(*The lights go down to black.*)

Act One

The lights come up on ROSE hanging up clothes. She hums and sings softly to herself. It is the following morning.

ROSE: (*Sings*) Jesus, be a fence all around me every day
Jesus, I want you to protect me as I travel
on my way.
Jesus, be a fence all around me every day.
(Troy enters from the house)

ROSE (*continued*): Jesus, I want you to protect me
As I travel on my way.

(*To* TROY)
'Morning. You ready for breakfast? I can fix it soon as I finish hanging up these clothes?

TROY: I got the coffee on. That'll be alright. I'll just drink some of that this morning.

ROSE: That 651 hit yesterday. That's the second time this month. Miss Pearl hit for a dollar . . . seem like those that need the least always get lucky. Poor folks can't get nothing.

TROY: Them numbers don't know nobody. I don't know why you fool with them. You and Lyons both.

ROSE: It's something to do.

TROY: You ain't doing nothing but throwing your money away.

ROSE: Troy, you know I don't play foolishly. I just play a nickel here and a nickel there.

TROY: That's two nickels you done thrown away.

ROSE: Now I hit sometimes . . . that makes up for it. It always comes in handy when I do hit. I don't hear you complaining then.

TROY: I ain't complaining now. I just say it's foolish. Trying to guess out of six hundred ways which way the number gonna come. If I had all the money niggers, these Negroes, throw away on numbers for one week—just one week—I'd be a rich man.

ROSE: Well, you wishing and calling it foolish ain't gonna stop folks from playing numbers. That's one thing for sure. Besides . . . some good things come from playing numbers. Look where Pope done bought him that restaurant off of numbers.

TROY: I can't stand niggers like that. Man ain't had two dimes to rub together. He walking around with his shoes all run over bumming money for cigarettes. Alright. Got lucky there and hit the numbers . . .

ROSE: Troy, I know all about it.

TROY: Had good sense, I'll say that for him. He ain't throwed his money away. I seen niggers hit the numbers and go through two thousand dollars in four days. Man brought him that restaurant down there . . . fixed it up real nice . . . and then didn't want nobody to come in it! A Negro go in there and can't get no kind of service. I seen a white fellow come in there and order a bowl of stew. Pope picked all the meat out the pot for him. Man ain't had nothing but a bowl of meat! Negro come behind him and ain't got nothing but the potatoes and carrots. Talking about what numbers do for people, you picked a wrong example. Ain't done nothing but make a worser fool out of him than he was before.

ROSE: Troy, you ought to stop worrying about what happened at work yesterday.

TROY: I ain't worried. Just told me to be down there at the Commissioner's office on Friday. Everybody think they gonna fire me. I ain't worried about them firing me. You ain't got to worry about that.
(*Pause.*)
Where's Cory? Cory in the house? (*Calls.*) Cory?

ROSE: He gone out.

TROY: Out, huh? He gone out 'cause he know I want him to help me with this fence. I know how he is. That boy scared of work.

(*GABRIEL enters. He comes halfway down the alley and, hearing Troy's voice, stops.*)

TROY (*continues*):   He ain't done a lick of work in his life.

ROSE: He had to go to football practice. Coach wanted them to get in a little extra practice before the season start.

TROY: I got his practice . . . running out of here before he get his chores done.

ROSE: Troy, what is wrong with you this morning? Don't nothing set right with you. Go on back in there and go to bed . . . get up on the other side.

TROY: Why something got to be wrong with me? I ain't said nothing wrong with me.

ROSE: You got something to say about everything. First it's the numbers . . . then it's the way the man runs his restaurant . . . then you done got on Cory. What's it gonna be next? Take a look up there and see if the weather suits you . . . or is it gonna be how you gonna put up the fence with the clothes hanging in the yard.

TROY: You hit the nail on the head then.

ROSE: I know you like I know the back of my hand. Go on in there and get you some coffee . . . see if that straighten you up. 'Cause you ain't right this morning.

(*TROY starts into the house and sees* GABRIEL. GABRIEL *starts singing.* TROY's *brother, he is seven years younger than* TROY. *Injured in World War II, he has a metal plate in his head. He carries an old trumpet tied around his waist and believes with every fiber of his being that he is the Archangel Gabriel. He carries a chipped basket with an assortment of discarded fruits and vegetables he has picked up in the strip district and which he attempts to sell.*)

GABRIEL: (*Singing.*)
Yes, ma'am, I got plums
You ask me how I sell them
Oh ten cents apiece
Three for a quarter
Come and buy now
'Cause I'm here today
And tomorrow I'll be gone

(*GABRIEL enters.*)

Hey, Rose!

ROSE: How you doing, Gabe?

GABRIEL: There's Troy . . . Hey, Troy!

TROY: Hey, Gabe.
(*Exit into kitchen.*)

ROSE: (*To GABRIEL.*) What you got there?

GABRIEL: You know what I got, Rose. I got fruits and vegetables.

ROSE: (*Looking in basket.*) Where's all these plums you talking about?

GABRIEL: I ain't got no plums today, Rose. I was just singing that. Have some tomorrow. Put me in a big order for plums. Have enough plums tomorrow for St. Peter and everybody.

(*TROY re-enters from kitchen, crosses to steps.*)
(*To ROSE.*)
Troy's mad at me.

TROY: I ain't mad at you. What I got to be mad at you about? You ain't done nothing to me.

GABRIEL: I just moved over to Miss Pearl's to keep out from in your way. I ain't mean no harm by it.

TROY: Who said anything about that? I ain't said anything about that.

GABRIEL: You ain't mad at me, is you?

TROY: Naw . . . I ain't mad at you, Gabe. If I was mad at you I'd tell you about it.

GABRIEL: Got me two rooms. In the basement. Got my own door too. Wanna see my key?
(*He holds up a key.*)
That's my own key! Ain't nobody else got a key like that. That's my key! My two rooms!

TROY: Well, that's good, Gabe. You got your own key . . . that's good.

ROSE: You hungry, Gabe? I was just fixing to cook Troy his breakfast.

GABRIEL: I'll take some biscuits. You got some biscuits? Did you know when I was in heaven . . . every morning me and St. Peter would sit down by the gate and eat some big fat biscuits? Oh, yeah! We had us a good time. We'd sit there and eat us them biscuits and then St. Peter would go off to sleep and tell me to wake him up when it's time to open the gates for the judgment.

ROSE: Well, come on . . . I'll make up a batch of biscuits.

(*ROSE exits into the house.*)

GABRIEL: Troy . . . St. Peter got your name in the book. I seen it. It say . . . Troy Maxson. I say . . . I know him! He got the same name like what I got. That's my brother!

TROY: How many times you gonna tell me that, Gabe?

GABRIEL: Ain't got my name in the book. Don't have to have my name. I done died and went to heaven. He got your name though. One morning St. Peter was looking at his book . . . marking it up for the judgment . . . and he let me see your name. Got it in there under M. Got Rose's name . . . I ain't seen it like I seen yours . . . but I know it's in there. He got a great big book. Got everybody's name what was ever been born. That's what he told me. But I seen your name. Seen it with my own eyes.

TROY: Go on in the house there. Rose going to fix you something to eat.

GABRIEL: Oh, I ain't hungry. I done had breakfast with Aunt Jemimah. She come by and cooked me up a whole mess of flapjacks. Remember how we used to eat them flapjacks?

TROY: Go on in the house and get you something to eat now.

GABRIEL: I got to go sell my plums. I done sold some tomatoes. Got me two quarters. Wanna see?
(*He shows* TROY *his quarters.*)
I'm gonna save them and buy me a new horn so St. Peter can hear me when it's time to open the gates.
(GABRIEL *stops suddenly. Listens.*)
Hear that? That's the hellhounds. I got to chase them out of here. Go on get out of here! Get out!
(GABRIEL *exits singing.*)
Better get ready for the judgment
Better get ready for the judgment
My Lord is coming down

(ROSE *enters from the house.*)

TROY: He gone off somewhere.

GABRIEL: (*Offstage*)
Better get ready for the judgment
Better get ready for the judgment morning
Better get ready for the judgment
My God is coming down

ROSE: He ain't eating right. Miss Pearl say she can't get him to eat nothing.

TROY: What you want me to do about it, Rose? I done did everything I can for the man. I can't make him get well. Man got half his head blown away . . . what you expect?

ROSE: Seem like something ought to be done to help him.

TROY: Man don't bother nobody. He just mixed up from

that metal plate he got in his head. Ain't no sense for him to go back into the hospital.

ROSE: Least he be eating right. They can help him take care of himself.

TROY: Don't nobody wanna be locked up, Rose. What you wanna lock him up for? Man go over there and fight the war . . . messin' around with them Japs, get half his head blown off . . . and they give him a lousy three thousand dollars. And I had to swoop down on that.

ROSE: Is you fixing to go into that again?

TROY: That's the only way I got a roof over my head . . . cause of that metal plate.

ROSE: Ain't no sense you blaming yourself for nothing. Gabe wasn't in no condition to manage that money. You done what was right by him. Can't nobody say you ain't done what was right by him. Look how long you took care of him . . . till he wanted to have his own place and moved over there with Miss Pearl.

TROY: That ain't what I'm saying, woman! I'm just stating the facts. If my brother didn't have that metal plate in his head . . . I wouldn't have a pot to piss in or a window to throw it out of. And I'm fifty-three years old. Now see if you can understand that!

(*TROY gets up from the porch and starts to exit the yard.*)

ROSE: Where you going off to? You been running out of here every Saturday for weeks. I thought you was gonna work on this fence?

TROY: I'm gonna walk down to Taylors'. Listen to the ball game. I'll be back in a bit. I'll work on it when I get back.

(*He exits the yard. The lights go to black.*)

The lights come up on the yard. It is four hours later. ROSE is taking down the clothes from the line. CORY enters carrying his football equipment.

ROSE: Your daddy like to had a fit with you running out of here this morning without doing your chores.

CORY: I told you I had to go to practice.

ROSE: He say you were supposed to help him with this fence.

CORY: He been saying that the last four or five Saturdays, and then he don't never do nothing, but go down to Taylors'. Did you tell him about the recruiter?

ROSE: Yeah, I told him.

CORY: What he say?

ROSE: He ain't said nothing too much. You get in there and get started on your chores before he gets back. Go on and scrub down them steps before he gets back here hollering and carrying on.

CORY: I'm hungry. What you got to eat, Mama?

ROSE: Go on and get started on your chores. I got some meat loaf in there. Go on and make you a sandwich . . . and don't leave no mess in there.
(*CORY exits into the house. ROSE continues to take down the clothes. TROY enters the yard and sneaks up and grabs her from behind.*)
Troy! Go on, now. You liked to scared me to death. What was the score of the game? Lucille had me on the phone and I couldn't keep up with it.

TROY: What I care about the game? Come here, woman. (*He tries to kiss her.*)

ROSE: I thought you went down Taylors' to listen to the game. Go on, Troy! You supposed to be putting up this fence.

TROY: (*Attempting to kiss her again.*) I'll put it up when I finish with what is at hand.

ROSE: Go on, Troy. I ain't studying you.

TROY: (*Chasing after her.*) I'm studying you . . . fixing to do my homework!

ROSE: Troy, you better leave me alone.

TROY: Where's Cory? That boy brought his butt home yet?

ROSE: He's in the house doing his chores.

TROY: (*Calling.*) Cory! Get your butt out here, boy!

(*ROSE exits into the house with the laundry. TROY goes over to the pile of wood, picks up a board, and starts sawing. CORY enters from the house.*)

TROY: You just now coming in here from leaving this morning?

CORY: Yeah, I had to go to football practice.

TROY: Yeah, what?

CORY: Yessir.

TROY: I ain't but two seconds off you noway. The garbage sitting in there overflowing . . . you ain't done none of your chores . . . and you come in here talking about "Yeah."

CORY: I was just getting ready to do my chores now, Pop . . .

TROY: Your first chore is to help me with this fence on Saturday. Everything else come after that. Now get that saw and cut them boards.

(*CORY takes the saw and begins cutting the boards. TROY continues working. There is a long pause.*)

CORY: Hey, Pop . . . why don't you buy a TV?

TROY: What I want with a TV? What I want one of them for?

CORY: Everybody got one. Earl, Ba Bra . . . Jesse!

TROY: I ain't asked you who had one. I say what I want with one?

CORY: So you can watch it. They got lots of things on TV. Baseball games and everything. We could watch the World Series.

TROY: Yeah . . . and how much this TV cost?

CORY: I don't know. They got them on sale for around two hundred dollars.

TROY: Two hundred dollars, huh?

CORY: That ain't that much, Pop.

TROY: Naw, it's just two hundred dollars. See that roof you got over your head at night? Let me tell you something about that roof. It's been over ten years since that roof was last tarred. See now . . . the snow come this winter and sit up there on that roof like it is . . . and it's gonna seep inside. It's just gonna be a little bit . . . ain't gonna hardly notice it. Then the next thing you know, it's gonna be leaking all over the house. Then the wood rot from all that water and you gonna need a whole new roof. Now, how much you think it cost to get that roof tarred?

CORY: I don't know.

TROY: Two hundred and sixty-four dollars . . . cash money. While you thinking about a TV, I got to be thinking about the roof . . . and whatever else go wrong around here. Now if you had two hundred dollars, what would you do . . . fix the roof or buy a TV?

CORY: I'd buy a TV. Then when the roof started to leak . . . when it needed fixing . . . I'd fix it.

TROY: Where you gonna get the money from? You done spent it for a TV. You gonna sit up and watch the water run all over your brand new TV.

CORY: Aw, Pop. You got money. I know you do.

TROY: Where I got it at, huh?

CORY: You got it in the bank.

TROY: You wanna see my bankbook? You wanna see that seventy-three dollars and twenty-two cents I got sitting up in there.

CORY: You ain't got to pay for it all at one time. You can put a down payment on it and carry it on home with you.

TROY: Not me. I ain't gonna owe nobody nothing if I can help it. Miss a payment and they come and snatch it right out your house. Then what you got? Now, soon as I get two hundred dollars clear, then I'll buy a TV. Right now, as soon as I get two hundred and sixty-four dollars, I'm gonna have this roof tarred.

CORY: Aw . . . Pop!

TROY: You go on and get you two hundred dollars and buy one if ya want it. I got better things to do with my money.

CORY: I can't get no two hundred dollars. I ain't never seen two hundred dollars.

TROY: I'll tell you what . . . you get you a hundred dollars and I'll put the other hundred with it.

CORY: Alright, I'm gonna show you.

TROY: You gonna show me how you can cut them boards right now.

(*CORY begins to cut the boards. There is a long pause.*)

CORY: The Pirates won today. That makes five in a row.

TROY: I ain't thinking about the Pirates. Got an all-white team. Got that boy . . . that Puerto Rican boy . . . Clemente. Don't even half-play him. That boy could be something if they give him a chance. Play him one day and sit him on the bench the next.

CORY: He gets a lot of chances to play.

TROY: I'm talking about playing regular. Playing every

day so you can get your timing. That's what I'm talking about.

CORY: They got some white guys on the team that don't play every day. You can't play everybody at the same time.

TROY: If they got a white fellow sitting on the bench . . . you can bet your last dollar he can't play! The colored guy got to be twice as good before he get on the team. That's why I don't want you to get all tied up in them sports. Man on the team and what it get him? They got colored on the team and don't use them. Same as not having them. All them teams the same.

CORY: The Braves got Hank Aaron and Wes Covington. Hank Aaron hit two home runs today. That makes forty-three.

TROY: Hank Aaron ain't nobody. That's what you supposed to do. That's how you supposed to play the game. Ain't nothing to it. It's just a matter of timing . . . getting the right follow-through. Hell, I can hit forty-three home runs right now!

CORY: Not off no major-league pitching, you couldn't.

TROY: We had better pitching in the Negro leagues. I hit seven home runs off of Satchel Paige. You can't get no better than that!

CORY: Sandy Koufax. He's leading the league in strike-outs.

TROY: I ain't thinking of no Sandy Koufax.

CORY: You got Warren Spahn and Lew Burdette. I bet you couldn't hit no home runs off of Warren Spahn.

TROY: I'm through with it now. You go on and cut them boards.

(*Pause.*)

Your mama tell me you done got recruited by a college football team? Is that right?

CORY: Yeah. Coach Zellman say the recruiter gonna be coming by to talk to you. Get you to sign the permission papers.

TROY: I thought you supposed to be working down there at the A&P. Ain't you suppose to be working down there after school?

CORY: Mr. Stawicki say he gonna hold my job for me until after the football season. Say starting next week I can work weekends.

TROY: I thought we had an understanding about this football stuff? You suppose to keep up with your chores and hold that job down at the A&P. Ain't been around here all day on a Saturday. Ain't none of your chores done . . . and now you telling me you done quit your job.

CORY: I'm gonna be working weekends.

TROY: You damn right you are! And ain't no need for nobody coming around here to talk to me about signing nothing.

CORY: Hey, Pop . . . you can't do that. He's coming all the way from North Carolina.

TROY: I don't care where he coming from. The white man ain't gonna let you get nowhere with that football noway. You go on and get your book-learning so you can work yourself up in that A&P or learn how to fix cars or build houses or something, get you a trade. That way you have something can't nobody take away from you. You go on and learn how to put your hands to some good use. Besides hauling people's garbage.

CORY: I get good grades, Pop. That's why the recruiter wants to talk with you. You got to keep up your grades to get recruited. This way I'll be going to college. I'll get a chance . . .

TROY: First you gonna get your butt down there to the A&P and get your job back.

CORY: Mr. Stawicki done already hired somebody else 'cause I told him I was playing football.

TROY: You a bigger fool than I thought . . . to let somebody take away your job so you can play some football. Where you gonna get your money to take out your girlfriend and whatnot? What kind of foolishness is that to let somebody take away your job?

CORY: I'm still gonna be working weekends.

TROY: Naw . . . naw. You getting your butt out of here and finding you another job.

CORY: Come on, Pop! I got to practice. I can't work after school and play football too. The team needs me. That's what Coach Zellman say . . .

TROY: I don't care what nobody else say. I'm the boss . . . you understand? I'm the boss around here. I do the only saying what counts.

CORY: Come on, Pop!

TROY: I asked you . . . did you understand?

CORY: Yeah . . .

TROY: What?!

CORY: Yessir.

TROY: You go on down there to that A&P and see if you can get your job back. If you can't do both . . . then you quit the football team. You've got to take the crookeds with the straights.

CORY: Yessir.
(*Pause.*)
Can I ask you a question?

TROY: What the hell you wanna ask me? Mr. Stawicki the one you got the questions for.

CORY: How come you ain't never liked me?

TROY: Liked you? Who the hell say I got to like you? What law is there say I got to like you? Wanna stand up in my face and ask a damn fool-ass question like that. Talking about liking somebody. Come here, boy, when I talk to you.
(*CORY comes over to where TROY is working. He stands slouched over and TROY shoves him on his shoulder.*)
Straighten up, goddammit! I asked you a question . . . what law is there say I got to like you?

CORY: None.

TROY: Well, alright then! Don't you eat every day?
(*Pause.*)
Answer me when I talk to you! Don't you eat every day?

CORY: Yeah.

TROY: Nigger, as long as you in my house, you put that sir on the end of it when you talk to me!

CORY: Yes . . . sir.

TROY: You eat every day.

CORY: Yessir!

TROY: Got a roof over your head.

CORY: Yessir!

TROY: Got clothes on your back.

CORY: Yessir.

TROY: Why you think that is?

CORY: Cause of you.

TROY: Aw, hell I know it's 'cause of me . . . but why do you think that is?

CORY: (*Hesitant.*) Cause you like me.

TROY: Like you? I go out of here every morning . . . bust my butt . . . putting up with them crackers every day . . . cause I like you? You about the biggest fool I ever saw.
(*Pause.*)
It's my job. It's my responsibility! You understand that? A man got to take care of his family. You live in my house . . . sleep you behind on my bedclothes . . . fill you belly up with my food . . . cause you my son. You my flesh and blood. Not 'cause I like you! Cause it's my duty to take care of you. I owe a responsibility to you! Let's get this straight right here . . . before it go along any further . . . I ain't got to like you. Mr. Rand don't give me my money come payday cause he likes me. He gives me cause he owe me. I done give you everything I had to give you. I gave you your life! Me and your mama worked that out between us. And liking your black ass wasn't part of the bargain. Don't you try and go through life worrying about if somebody like you or not. You best be making sure they doing right by you. You understand what I'm saying, boy?

CORY: Yessir.

TROY: Then get the hell out of my face, and get on down to that A&P.

(*ROSE has been standing behind the screen door for much of the scene. She enters as CORY exits.*)

ROSE: Why don't you let the boy go ahead and play football, Troy? Ain't no harm in that. He's just trying to be like you with the sports.

TROY: I don't want him to be like me! I want him to move as far away from my life as he can get. You the only decent thing that ever happened to me. I wish him that. But I don't wish him a thing else from my life. I decided seventeen years ago that boy wasn't getting involved in no sports. Not after what they did to me in the sports.

ROSE: Troy, why don't you admit you was too old to play in the major leagues? For once . . . why don't you admit that?

TROY: What do you mean too old? Don't come telling me I was too old. I just wasn't the right color. Hell, I'm fifty-three years old and can do better than Selkirk's .269 right now!

ROSE: How's was you gonna play ball when you were over forty? Sometimes I can't get no sense out of you.

TROY: I got good sense, woman. I got sense enough not to let my boy get hurt over playing no sports. You been mothering that boy too much. Worried about if people like him.

ROSE: Everything that boy do . . . he do for you. He wants you to say "Good job, son." That's all.

TROY: Rose, I ain't got time for that. He's alive. He's healthy. He's got to make his own way. I made mine. Ain't nobody gonna hold his hand when he get out there in that world.

ROSE: Times have changed from when you was young, Troy. People change. The world's changing around you and you can't even see it.

TROY: (*Slow, methodical.*) Woman . . . I do the best I can do. I come in here every Friday. I carry a sack of potatoes and a bucket of lard. You all line up at the door with your hands out. I give you the lint from my pockets. I give you my sweat and my blood. I ain't got no tears. I done spent them. We go upstairs in that room at night . . . and I fall down on you and try to blast a hole into forever. I get up Monday morning . . . find my lunch on the table. I go out. Make my way. Find my strength to carry me through to the next Friday.
(*Pause.*)
That's all I got, Rose. That's all I got to give. I can't give nothing else.

(*TROY exits into the house. The lights go down to black.*)

It is Friday. Two weeks later. CORY *starts out of the house with his football equipment. The phone rings.*

CORY: (*Calling.*) I got it!
(*He answers the phone and stands in the screen door talking.*)
Hello? Hey, Jesse. Naw . . . I was just getting ready to leave now.

ROSE: (*Calling.*) Cory!

CORY: I told you, man, them spikes is all tore up. You can use them if you want, but they ain't no good. Earl got some spikes.

ROSE: (*Calling.*) Cory!

CORY: (*Calling to* ROSE.) Mam? I'm talking to Jesse.
(*Into phone.*)
When she say that? (*Pause.*) Aw, you lying, man. I'm gonna tell her you said that.

ROSE: (*Calling.*) Cory, don't you go nowhere!

CORY: I got to go to the game, Ma!
(*Into the phone.*)

Yeah, hey, look, I'll talk to you later. Yeah, I'll meet you over Earl's house. Later. Bye, Ma.

(*CORY exits the house and starts out the yard.*)

ROSE: Cory, where you going off to? You got that stuff all pulled out and thrown all over your room.

CORY: (*In the yard.*) I was looking for my spikes. Jesse wanted to borrow my spikes.

ROSE: Get up there and get that cleaned up before your daddy get back in here.

CORY: I got to go to the game! I'll clean it up *when I get back.*

(*CORY exits.*)

ROSE: That's all he need to do is see that room all messed up.

(*ROSE exits into the house. TROY and BONO enter the yard. TROY is dressed in clothes other than his work clothes.*)

BONO: He told him the same thing he told you. Take it to the union.

TROY: Brownie ain't got that much sense. Man wasn't thinking about nothing. He wait until I confront them on it . . . then he wanna come crying seniority.
(*Calls.*)
Hey, Rose!

BONO: I wish I could have seen Mr. Rand's face when he told you.

TROY: He couldn't get it out of his mouth! Liked to bit his tongue! When they called me down there to the Commis-

sioner's office . . . he thought they was gonna fire me.
Like everybody else.

BONO: I didn't think they was gonna fire you. I thought
they was gonna put you on the warning paper.

TROY: Hey, Rose!
(*To BONO.*)
Yeah, Mr. Rand like to bit his tongue.
(*TROY breaks the seal on the bottle, takes a drink, and
hands it to BONO.*)

BONO: I see you run right down to Taylors' and told that
Alberta gal.

TROY: (*Calling.*) Hey Rose! (*To BONO.*) I told everybody.
Hey, Rose! I went down there to cash my check.

ROSE: (*Entering from the house.*) Hush all that hollering,
man! I know you out here. What they say down there at
the Commissioner's office?

TROY: You supposed to come when I call you, woman.
Bono'll tell you that.
(*To BONO.*)
Don't Lucille come when you call her?

ROSE: Man, hush your mouth. I ain't no dog . . . talk
about "come when you call me."

TROY: (*Puts his arm around ROSE.*) You hear this, Bono?
I had me an old dog used to get uppity like that. You say,
"C'mere, Blue!" . . . and he just lay there and look at
you. End up getting a stick and chasing him away trying
to make him come.

ROSE: I ain't studying you and your dog. I remember you
used to sing that old song.

TROY: (*He sings.*) Hear it ring! Hear it ring!
I had a dog his name was Blue.

ROSE: Don't nobody wanna hear you sing that old song.

TROY: (*Sings.*) You know Blue was mighty true.

ROSE: Used to have Cory running around here singing that song.

BONO: Hell, I remember that song myself.

TROY: (*Sings.*) You know Blue was a good old dog.
Blue treed a possum in a hollow log.

That was my daddy's song. My daddy made up that song.

ROSE: I don't care who made it up. Don't nobody wanna hear you sing it.

TROY: (*Makes a song like calling a dog.*) Come here, woman.

ROSE: You come in here carrying on, I reckon they ain't fired you. What they say down there at the Commissioner's office?

TROY: Look here, Rose . . . Mr. Rand called me into his office today when I got back from talking to them people down there . . . it come from up top . . . he called me in and told me they was making me a driver.

ROSE: Troy, you kidding!

TROY: No I ain't. Ask Bono.

ROSE: Well, that's great, Troy. Now you don't have to hassle them people no more.

(*LYONS enters from the street.*)

TROY: Aw hell, I wasn't looking to see you today. I thought you was in jail. Got it all over the front page of the *Courier* about them raiding Sefus' place . . . where you be hanging out with all them thugs.

LYONS: Hey, Pop . . . that ain't got nothing to do with me. I don't go down there gambling. I go down there to sit in with the band. I ain't got nothing to do with the gambling part. They got some good music down there.

TROY: They got some rogues . . . is what they got.

LYONS: How you been, Mr. Bono? Hi, Rose.

BONO: I see where you playing down at the Crawford Grill tonight.

ROSE: How come you ain't brought Bonnie like I told you. You should have brought Bonnie with you, she ain't been over in a month of Sundays.

LYONS: I was just in the neighborhood . . . thought I'd stop by.

TROY: Here he come . . .

BONO: Your daddy got a promotion on the rubbish. He's gonna be the first colored driver. Ain't got to do nothing but sit up there and read the paper like them white fellows.

LYONS: Hey, Pop . . . if you knew how to read you'd be alright.

BONO: Naw . . . naw . . . you mean if the nigger knew how to *drive* he'd be all right. Been fighting with them people about driving and ain't even got a license. Mr. Rand know you ain't got no driver's license?

TROY: Driving ain't nothing. All you do is point the truck where you want it to go. Driving ain't nothing.

BONO: Do Mr. Rand know you ain't got no driver's license? That's what I'm talking about. I ain't asked if driving was easy. I asked if Mr. Rand know you ain't got no driver's license.

TROY: He ain't got to know. The man ain't got to know my business. Time he find out, I have two or three driver's licenses.

LYONS: (*Going into his pocket.*) Say, look here, Pop . . .

TROY: I knew it was coming. Didn't I tell you, Bono? I know what kind of "Look here, Pop" that was. The nigger fixing to ask me for some money. It's Friday night. It's my payday. All them rogues down there on the avenue . . . the ones that ain't in jail . . . and Lyons is hopping in his shoes to get down there with them

LYONS: See, Pop . . . if you give somebody else a chance to talk sometime, you'd see that I was fixing to pay you back your ten dollars like I told you. Here . . . I told you I'd pay you when Bonnie got paid.

TROY: Naw . . . you go ahead and keep that ten dollars. Put it in the bank. The next time you feel like you wanna come by here and ask me for something . . . you go on down there and get that.

LYONS: Here's your ten dollars, Pop. I told you I don't want you to give me nothing. I just wanted to borrow ten dollars.

TROY: Naw . . . you go on and keep that for the next time you want to ask me.

LYONS: Come on, Pop . . . here go your ten dollars.

ROSE: Why don't you go on and let the boy pay you back, Troy?

LYONS: Here you go, Rose. If you don't take it I'm gonna have to hear about it for the next six months.
(*He hands her the money.*)

ROSE: You can hand yours over here too, Troy.

TROY: You see this, Bono. You see how they do me.

BONO: Yeah, Lucille do me the same way.

(*GABRIEL is heard singing offstage. He enters.*)

GABRIEL: Better get ready for the Judgment! Better get ready for . . . Hey! . . . Hey! . . . There's Troy's boy!

LYONS: How you doing, Uncle Gabe?

GABRIEL: Lyons . . . The King of the Jungle! Rose . . . hey, Rose. Got a flower for you.
(*He takes a rose from his pocket.*)
Picked it myself. That's the same rose like you is!

ROSE: That's right nice of you, Gabe.

LYONS: What you been doing, Uncle Gabe?

GABRIEL: Oh, I been chasing hellhounds and waiting on the time to tell St. Peter to open the gates.

LYONS: You been chasing hellhounds, huh? Well . . . you doing the right thing, Uncle Gabe. Somebody got to chase them.

GABRIEL: Oh, yeah . . . I know it. The devil's strong. The devil ain't no pushover. Hellhounds snipping at everybody's heels. But I got my trumpet waiting on the judgment time.

LYONS: Waiting on the Battle of Armageddon, huh?

GABRIEL: Ain't gonna be too much of a battle when God get to waving that Judgment sword. But the people's gonna have a hell of a time trying to get into heaven if them gates ain't open.

LYONS: (*Putting his arm around* GABRIEL.) You hear this, Pop. Uncle Gabe, you alright!

GABRIEL: (*Laughing with* LYONS.) Lyons! King of the Jungle.

ROSE: You gonna stay for supper, Gabe. Want me to fix you a plate?

GABRIEL: I'll take a sandwich, Rose. Don't want no plate. Just wanna eat with my hands. I'll take a sandwich.

ROSE: How about you, Lyons? You staying? Got some short ribs cooking.

LYONS: Naw, I won't eat nothing till after we finished playing.
(*Pause.*)
You ought to come down and listen to me play, Pop.

TROY: I don't like that Chinese music. All that noise.

ROSE: Go on in the house and wash up, Gabe . . . I'll fix you a sandwich.

GABRIEL: (*To* LYONS, *as he exits.*) Troy's mad at me.

LYONS: What you mad at Uncle Gabe for, Pop.

ROSE: He thinks Troy's mad at him cause he moved over to Miss Pearl's.

TROY: I ain't mad at the man. He can live where he want to live at.

LYONS: What he move over there for? Miss Pearl don't like nobody.

ROSE: She don't mind him none. She treats him real nice. She just don't allow all that singing.

TROY: She don't mind that rent he be paying . . . that's what she don't mind.

ROSE: Troy, I ain't going through that with you no more. He's over there cause he want to have his own place. He can come and go as he please.

TROY: Hell, he could come and go as he please here. I wasn't stopping him. I ain't put no rules on him.

ROSE: It ain't the same thing, Troy. And you know it.
(*GABRIEL comes to the door.*)
Now, that's the last I wanna hear about that. I don't wanna hear nothing else about Gabe and Miss Pearl. And next week . . .

GABRIEL: I'm ready for my sandwich, Rose.

ROSE: And next week . . . when that recruiter come from that school . . . I want you to sign that paper and go on and let Cory play football. Then that'll be the last I have to hear about that.

TROY: (*To ROSE as she exits into the house.*) I ain't thinking about Cory nothing.

LYONS: What . . . Cory got recruited? What school he going to?

TROY: That boy walking around here smelling his piss . . . thinking he's grown. Thinking he's gonna do what he want, irrespective of what I say. Look here, Bono . . . I left the Commissioner's office and went down to the A&P . . . that boy ain't working down there. He lying to me. Telling me he got his job back . . . telling me he working weekends . . . telling me he working after school . . . Mr. Stawicki tell me he ain't working down there at all!

LYONS: Cory just growing up. He's just busting at the seams trying to fill out your shoes.

TROY: I don't care what he's doing. When he get to the point where he wanna disobey me . . . then it's time for him to move on. Bono'll tell you that. I bet he ain't never disobeyed his daddy without paying the consequences.

BONO: I ain't never had a chance. My daddy came on through . . . but I ain't never knew him to see him . . . or what he had on his mind or where he went. Just moving on through. Searching out the New Land. That's what the old folks used to call it. See a fellow moving around from place to place . . . woman to woman . . . called it searching out the New Land. I can't say if he ever found it. I come along, didn't want no kids. Didn't know if I was gonna be in one place long enough to fix on them right as their daddy. I figured I was going searching too. As it turned out I been hooked up with Lucille near about as long as your daddy been with Rose. Going on sixteen years.

TROY: Sometimes I wish I hadn't known my daddy. He ain't cared nothing about no kids. A kid to him wasn't nothing. All he wanted was for you to learn how to walk so he could start you to working. When it come time for eating . . . he ate first. If there was anything left over, that's what you got. Man would sit down and eat two chickens and give you the wing.

LYONS: You ought to stop that, Pop. Everybody feed their kids. No matter how hard times is . . . everybody care about their kids. Make sure they have something to eat.

TROY: The only thing my daddy cared about was getting them bales of cotton in to Mr. Lubin. That's the only thing that mattered to him. Sometimes I used to wonder why he was living. Wonder why the devil hadn't come and got him. "Get them bales of cotton in to Mr. Lubin" and find out he owe him money . . .

LYONS: He should have just went on and left when he saw he couldn't get nowhere. That's what I would have done.

TROY: How he gonna leave with eleven kids? And where he gonna go? He ain't knew how to do nothing but farm. No, he was trapped and I think he knew it. But I'll say this for him . . . he felt a responsibility toward us. Maybe he ain't treated us the way I felt he should have . . . but without that responsibility he could have walked off and left us . . . made his own way.

BONO: A lot of them did. Back in those days what you talking about . . . they walk out their front door and just take on down one road or another and keep on walking.

LYONS: There you go! That's what I'm talking about.

BONO: Just keep on walking till you come to something else. Ain't you never heard of nobody having the walking blues? Well, that's what you call it when you just take off like that.

TROY: My daddy ain't had them walking blues! What you talking about? He stayed right there with his family. But he was just as evil as he could be. My mama couldn't stand him. Couldn't stand that evilness. She run off when I was about eight. She sneaked off one night after he had gone to sleep. Told me she was coming back for me. I ain't never seen her no more. All his women run off and left him. He wasn't good for nobody.
When my turn come to head out, I was fourteen and got

to sniffing around Joe Canewell's daughter. Had us an
old mule we called Greyboy. My daddy sent me out to
do some plowing and I tied up Greyboy and went to
fooling around with Joe Canewell's daughter. We done
found us a nice little spot, got real cozy with each other.
She about thirteen and we done figured we was grown
anyway . . . so we down there enjoying ourselves . . .
ain't thinking about nothing. We didn't know Greyboy
had got loose and wandered back to the house and my
daddy was looking for me. We down there by the creek
enjoying ourselves when my daddy come up on us. Surprised us. He had them leather straps off the mule and
commenced to whupping me like there was no tomorrow.
I jumped up, mad and embarrassed. I was scared of my
daddy. When he commenced to whupping on me . . .
quite naturally I run to get out of the way.
(*Pause.*)
Now I thought he was mad cause I ain't done my work.
But I see where he was chasing me off so he could have
the gal for himself. When I see what the matter of it was,
I lost all fear of my daddy. Right there is where I become
a man . . . at fourteen years of age.
(*Pause.*)
Now it was my turn to run him off. I picked up them
same reins that he had used on me. I picked up them
reins and commenced to whupping on him. The gal
jumped up and run off . . . and when my daddy turned
to face me, I could see why the devil had never come to
get him . . . cause he was the devil himself. I don't know
what happened. When I woke up, I was laying right there
by the creek, and Blue . . . this old dog we had . . . was
licking my face. I thought I was blind. I couldn't see
nothing. Both my eyes were swollen shut. I layed there
and cried. I didn't know what I was gonna do. The only
thing I knew was the time had come for me to leave my

daddy's house. And right there the world suddenly got big. And it was a long time before I could cut it down to where I could handle it.

Part of that cutting down was when I got to the place where I could feel him kicking in my blood and knew that the only thing that separated us was the matter of a few years.

(*GABRIEL enters from the house with a sandwich.*)

LYONS: What you got there, Uncle Gabe?

GABRIEL: Got me a ham sandwich. Rose gave me a ham sandwich.

TROY: I don't know what happened to him. I done lost touch with everybody except Gabriel. But I hope he's dead. I hope he found some peace.

LYONS: That's a heavy story, Pop. I didn't know you left home when you was fourteen.

TROY: And didn't know nothing. The only part of the world I knew was the forty-two acres of Mr. Lubin's land. That's all I knew about life.

LYONS: Fourteen's kinda young to be out on your own. (*Phone rings.*) I don't even think I was ready to be out on my own at fourteen. I don't know what I would have done.

TROY: I got up from the creek and walked on down to Mobile. I was through with farming. Figured I could do better in the city. So I walked the two hundred miles to Mobile.

LYONS: Wait a minute . . . you ain't walked no two hundred miles, Pop. Ain't nobody gonna walk no two hundred miles. You talking about some walking there.

BONO: That's the only way you got anywhere back in them days.

LYONS: Shhh. Damn if I wouldn't have hitched a ride with somebody!

TROY: Who you gonna hitch it with? They ain't had no cars and things like they got now. We talking about 1918.

ROSE: (*Entering*.) What you all out here getting into?

TROY: (*To* ROSE.) I'm telling Lyons how good he got it. He don't know nothing about this I'm talking.

ROSE: Lyons, that was Bonnie on the phone. She say you supposed to pick her up.

LYONS: Yeah, okay, Rose.

TROY: I walked on down to Mobile and hitched up with some of them fellows that was heading this way. Got up here and found out . . . not only couldn't you get a job . . . you couldn't find no place to live. I thought I was in freedom. Shhh. Colored folks living down there on the riverbanks in whatever kind of shelter they could find for themselves. Right down there under the Brady Street Bridge. Living in shacks made of sticks and tarpaper. Messed around there and went from bad to worse. Started stealing. First it was food. Then I figured, hell, if I steal money I can buy me some food. Buy me some shoes too! One thing led to another. Met your mama. I was young and anxious to be a man. Met your mama and had you. What I do that for? Now I got to worry about feeding you and her. Got to steal three times as much. Went out one day looking for somebody to rob . . . that's what I was, a robber. I'll tell you the truth. I'm ashamed of it today. But it's the truth. Went to rob this fellow . . . pulled out my knife . . . and he pulled out a gun. Shot me in the chest. It felt just like somebody had taken a hot branding iron and laid it on me. When he shot me I jumped at him with my knife. They told me I killed him and they put me in the penitentiary and locked me up for fifteen years. That's where I met Bono. That's where I learned how to play baseball. Got out that place and your mama had taken you and went on to make life without me. Fifteen years was a long time for her to wait. But that fifteen years cured me of that robbing stuff. Rose'll tell you. She asked me when I met her if I had gotten all that foolishness out of my system. And I told her, "Baby, it's you and baseball all what count with me." You hear me, Bono? I meant it too. She say, "Which one comes first?" I told her, "Baby, ain't no doubt it's baseball . . . but you stick and get old with me and we'll both outlive this baseball." Am I right, Rose? And it's true.

ROSE: Man, hush your mouth. You ain't said no such thing. Talking about, "Baby, you know you'll always be number one with me." That's what you was talking.

TROY: You hear that, Bono. That's why I love her.

BONO: Rose'll keep you straight. You get off the track, she'll straighten you up.

ROSE: Lyons, you better get on up and get Bonnie. She waiting on you.

LYONS: (*Gets up to go.*) Hey, Pop, why don't you come on down to the Grill and hear me play?

TROY: I ain't going down there. I'm too old to be sitting around in them clubs.

BONO: You got to be good to play down at the Grill.

LYONS: Come on, Pop . . .

TROY: I got to get up in the morning.

LYONS: You ain't got to stay long.

TROY: Naw, I'm gonna get my supper and go on to bed.

LYONS: Well, I got to go. I'll see you again.

TROY: Don't you come around my house on my payday.

ROSE: Pick up the phone and let somebody know you coming. And bring Bonnie with you. You know I'm always glad to see her.

LYONS: Yeah, I'll do that, Rose. You take care now. See you, Pop. See you, Mr. Bono. See you, Uncle Gabe.

GABRIEL: Lyons! King of the Jungle!

(*LYONS exits.*)

TROY: Is supper ready, woman? Me and you got some business to take care of. I'm gonna tear it up too.

ROSE: Troy, I done told you now!

TROY: (*Puts his arm around BONO.*) Aw hell, woman . . . this is Bono. Bono like family. I done known this nigger since . . . how long I done know you?

BONO: It's been a long time.

TROY: I done known this nigger since Skippy was a pup. Me and him done been through some times.

BONO: You sure right about that.

TROY: Hell, I done know him longer than I known you. And we still standing shoulder to shoulder. Hey, look here, Bono . . . a man can't ask for no more than that. (*Drinks to him.*)
I love you, nigger.

BONO: Hell, I love you too . . . but I got to get home see my woman. You got yours in hand. I got to go get mine.

(*BONO starts to exit as CORY enters the yard, dressed in his football uniform. He gives TROY a hard, uncompromising look.*)

CORY: What you do that for, Pop?
(*He throws his helmet down in the direction of TROY.*)

ROSE: What's the matter? Cory . . . what's the matter?

CORY: Papa done went up to the school and told Coach Zellman I can't play football no more. Wouldn't even let me play the game. Told him to tell the recruiter not to come.

ROSE: Troy . . .

TROY: What you Troying me for. Yeah, I did it. And the boy know why I did it.

CORY: Why you wanna do that to me? That was the one chance I had.

ROSE: Ain't nothing wrong with Cory playing football, Troy.

TROY: The boy lied to me. I told the nigger if he wanna play football . . . to keep up his chores and hold down that job at the A&P. That was the conditions. Stopped down there to see Mr. Stawicki . . .

CORY: I can't work after school during the football season, Pop! I tried to tell you that Mr. Stawicki's holding my job for me. You don't never want to listen to nobody. And then you wanna go and do this to me!

TROY: I ain't done nothing to you. You done it to yourself.

CORY: Just cause you didn't have a chance! You just scared I'm gonna be better than you, that's all.

TROY: Come here.

ROSE: Troy . . .

(*CORY reluctantly crosses over to TROY.*)

TROY: Alright! See. You done made a mistake.

CORY: I didn't even do nothing!

TROY: I'm gonna tell you what your mistake was. See . . . you swung at the ball and didn't hit it. That's strike one. See, you in the batter's box now. You swung and you missed. That's strike one. Don't you strike out!

(*Lights fade to black.*)

Act Two

The following morning. CORY is at the tree hitting the ball with the bat. He tries to mimic TROY, but his swing is awkward, less sure. ROSE enters from the house.

ROSE: Cory, I want you to help me with this cupboard.

CORY: I ain't quitting the team. I don't care what Poppa say.

ROSE: I'll talk to him when he gets back. He had to go see about your Uncle Gabe. The police done arrested him. Say he was disturbing the peace. He'll be back directly. Come on in here and help me clean out the top of this cupboard.

(CORY exits into the house. ROSE sees TROY and BONO coming down the alley.)

Troy . . . what they say down there?

TROY: Ain't said nothing. I give them fifty dollars and they let him go. I'll talk to you about it. Where's Cory?

ROSE: He's in there helping me clean out these cupboards.

TROY: Tell him to get his butt out here.

(TROY and BONO go over to the pile of wood. BONO picks up the saw and begins sawing.)

TROY: (*To* BONO.) All they want is the money. That makes six or seven times I done went down there and got him. See me coming they stick out their *hands*.

BONO: Yeah. I know what you mean. That's all they care about . . . that money. They don't care about what's right.
(*Pause.*)
Nigger, why you got to go and get some hard wood? You ain't doing nothing but building a little old fence. Get you some soft pine wood. That's all you need.

TROY: I know what I'm doing. This is outside wood. You put pine wood inside the house. Pine wood is inside wood. This here is outside wood. Now you tell me where the fence is gonna be?

BONO: You don't need this wood. You can put it up with pine wood and it'll stand as long as you gonna be here looking at it.

TROY: How you know how long I'm gonna be here, nigger? Hell, I might just live forever. Live longer than old man Horsely.

BONO: That's what Magee used to say.

TROY: Magee's a damn fool. Now you tell me who you ever heard of gonna pull their own teeth with a pair of rusty pliers.

BONO: The old folks . . . my granddaddy used to pull his teeth with pliers. They ain't had no dentists for the colored folks back then.

TROY: Get clean pliers! You understand? Clean pliers! Sterilize them! Besides we ain't living back then. All Magee had to do was walk over to Doc Goldblums.

BONO: I see where you and that Tallahassee gal . . . that Alberta . . . I see where you all done got tight.

TROY: What you mean "got tight"?

BONO: I see where you be laughing and joking with her all the time.

TROY: I laughs and jokes with all of them, Bono. You know me.

BONO: That ain't the kind of laughing and joking I'm talking about.

(*CORY enters from the house.*)

CORY: How you doing, Mr. Bono?

TROY: Cory? Get that saw from Bono and cut some wood. He talking about the wood's too hard to cut. Stand back there, Jim, and let that young boy show you how it's done.

BONO: He's sure welcome to it.
(*CORY takes the saw and begins to cut the wood.*)
Whew-e-e! Look at that. Big old strong boy. Look like Joe Louis. Hell, must be getting old the way I'm watching that boy whip through that wood.

CORY: I don't see why Mama want a fence around the yard noways.

TROY: Damn if I know either. What the hell she keeping out with it? She ain't got nothing nobody want.

BONO: Some people build fences to keep people out . . . and other people build fences to keep people in. Rose wants to hold on to you all. She loves you.

TROY: Hell, nigger, I don't need nobody to tell me my

wife loves me, Cory . . . go on in the house and see if you can find that other saw.

CORY: Where's it at?

TROY: I said find it! Look for it till you find it!
(*CORY exits into the house.*)
What's that supposed to mean? Wanna keep us in?

BONO: Troy . . . I done known you seem like damn near my whole life. You and Rose both. I done know both of you all for a long time. I remember when you met Rose. When you was hitting them baseball out the park. A lot of them old gals was after you then. You had the pick of the litter. When you picked Rose, I was happy for you. That was the first time I knew you had any sense. I said . . . My man Troy knows what he's doing . . . I'm gonna follow this nigger . . . he might take me somewhere. I been following you too. I done learned a whole heap of things about life watching you. I done learned how to tell where the shit lies. How to tell it from the alfalfa. You done learned me a lot of things. You showed me how to not make the same mistakes . . . to take life as it comes along and keep putting one foot in front of the other.
(*Pause.*)
Rose a good woman, Troy.

TROY: Hell, nigger, I know she a good woman. I been married to her for eighteen years. What you got on your mind, Bono?

BONO: I just say she a good woman. Just like I say anything. I ain't got to have nothing on my mind.

TROY: You just gonna say she a good woman and leave it hanging out there like that? Why you telling me she a good woman?

BONO: She loves you, Troy. Rose loves you.

TROY: You saying I don't measure up. That's what you trying to say. I don't measure up cause I'm seeing this other gal. I know what you trying to say.

BONO: I know what Rose means to you, Troy. I'm just trying to say I don't want to see you mess up.

TROY: Yeah, I appreciate that, Bono. If you was messing around on Lucille I'd be telling you the same thing.

BONO: Well, that's all I got to say. I just say that because I love you both.

TROY: Hell, you know me . . . I wasn't out there looking for nothing. You can't find a better woman than Rose. I know that. But seems like this woman just stuck onto me where I can't shake her loose. I done wrestled with it, tried to throw her off me . . . but she just stuck on tighter. Now she's stuck on for good.

BONO: You's in control . . . that's what you tell me all the time. You responsible for what you do.

TROY: I ain't ducking the responsibility of it. As long as it sets right in my heart . . . then I'm okay. Cause that's all I listen to. It'll tell me right from wrong every time. And I ain't talking about doing Rose no bad turn. I love Rose. She done carried me a long ways and I love and respect her for that.

BONO: I know you do. That's why I don't want to see you hurt her. But what you gonna do when she find out? What you got then? If you try and juggle both of them . . . sooner or later you gonna drop one of them. That's common sense.

TROY: Yeah, I hear what you saying, Bono. I been trying to figure a way to work it out.

BONO: Work it out right, Troy. I don't want to be getting all up between you and Rose's business . . . but work it so it come out right.

TROY: Aw hell, I get all up between you and Lucille's business. When you gonna get that woman that refrigerator she been wanting? Don't tell me you ain't got no money now. I know who your banker is. Mellon don't need that money bad as Lucille want that refrigerator. I'll tell you that.

BONO: Tell you what I'll do . . . when you finish building this fence for Rose . . . I'll buy Lucille that refrigerator.

TROY: You done stuck your foot in your mouth now!
(*TROY grabs up a board and begins to saw. BONO starts to walk out the yard.*)
Hey, nigger . . . where you going?

BONO: I'm going home. I know you don't expect me to help you now. I'm protecting my money. I wanna see you put that fence up by yourself. That's what I want to see. You'll be here another six months without me.

TROY: Nigger, you ain't right.

BONO: When it comes to my money . . . I'm right as fireworks on the Fourth of July.

TROY: Alright, we gonna see now. You better get out your bankbook.

(*BONO exits, and TROY continues to work. ROSE enters from the house.*)

ROSE: What they say down there? What's happening with Gabe?

TROY: I went down there and got him out. Cost me fifty dollars. Say he was disturbing the peace. Judge set up a hearing for him in three weeks. Say to show cause why he shouldn't be re-committed.

ROSE: What was he doing that cause them to arrest him?

TROY: Some kids was teasing him and he run them off home. Say he was howling and carrying on. Some folks seen him and called the police. That's all it was.

ROSE: Well, what's you say? What'd you tell the judge?

TROY: Told him I'd look after him. It didn't make no sense to recommit the man. He stuck out his big greasy palm and told me to give him fifty dollars and take him on home.

ROSE: Where's he at now? Where'd he go off to?

TROY: He's gone on about his business. He don't need nobody to hold his hand.

ROSE: Well, I don't know. Seem like that would be the best place for him if they did put him into the hospital. I know what you're gonna say. But that's what I think would be best.

TROY: The man done had his life ruined fighting for what? And they wanna take and lock him up. Let him be free. He don't bother nobody.

ROSE: Well, everybody got their own way of looking at it I guess. Come on and get your lunch. I got a bowl of lima beans and some cornbread in the oven. Come on get something to eat. Ain't no sense you fretting over Gabe. (ROSE turns to go into the house.)

TROY: Rose . . . got something to tell you.

ROSE: Well, come on . . . wait till I get this food on the table.

TROY: Rose!
(She stops and turns around.)
I don't know how to say this.
(Pause.)
I can't explain it none. It just sort of grows on you till it gets out of hand. It starts out like a little bush . . . and the next think you know it's a whole forest.

ROSE: Troy . . . what is you talking about?

TROY: I'm talking, woman, let me talk. I'm trying to find a way to tell you . . . I'm gonna be a daddy. I'm gonna be somebody's daddy.

ROSE: Troy . . . you're not telling me this? You're gonna be . . . what?

TROY: Rose . . . now . . . see . . .

ROSE: You telling me you gonna be somebody's daddy? You telling your *wife* this?

(GABRIEL enters from the street. He carries a rose in his hand.)

GABRIEL: Hey, Troy! Hey, Rose!

ROSE: I have to wait eighteen years to hear something like this.

GABRIEL: Hey, Rose . . . I got a flower for you.
(He hands it to her.)
That's a rose. Same rose like you is.

ROSE: Thanks, Gabe.

GABRIEL: Troy, you ain't mad at me is you? Them bad mens come and put me away. You ain't mad at me is you?

TROY: Naw, Gabe, I ain't mad at you.

ROSE: Eighteen years and you wanna come with this.

GABRIEL: (*Takes a quarter out of his pocket.*) See what I got? Got a brand new quarter.

TROY: Rose . . . it's just . . .

ROSE: Ain't nothing you can say, Troy. Ain't no way of explaining that.

GABRIEL: Fellow that give me this quarter had a whole mess of them. I'm gonna keep this quarter till it stop shining.

ROSE: Gabe, go on in the house there. I got some watermelon in the frigidaire. Go on and get you a piece.

GABRIEL: Say, Rose . . . you know I was chasing hellhounds and them bad mens come and get me and take me away. Troy helped me. He come down there and told them they better let me go before he beat them up. Yeah, he did!

ROSE: You go on and get you a piece of watermelon, Gabe. Them bad mens is gone now.

GABRIEL: Okay, Rose . . . gonna get me some watermelon. The kind with the stripes on it.
(*GABRIEL exits into the house.*)

ROSE: Why, Troy? Why? After all these years to come dragging this in to me now. It don't make no sense at your age. I could have expected this ten or fifteen years ago, but not now.

TROY: Age ain't got nothing to do with it, Rose.

ROSE: I done tried to be everything a wife should be. Everything a wife could be. Been married eighteen years and I got to live to see the day you tell me you been seeing another woman and done fathered a child by her.

And you know I ain't never wanted no half nothing in my family. My whole family is half. Everybody got different fathers and mothers . . . my two sisters and my brother. Can't hardly tell who's who. Can't never sit down and talk about Papa and Mama. It's your papa and your mama and my papa and my mama . . .

TROY: Rose . . . stop it now.

ROSE: I ain't never wanted that for none of my children. And now you wanna drag your behind in here and tell me something like this.

TROY: You ought to know. It's time for you to know.

ROSE: Well, I don't want to know, goddamn it!

TROY: I can't just make it go away. It's done now. I can't wish the circumstance of the thing away.

ROSE: And you don't want to either. Maybe you want to wish me and my boy away. Maybe that's what you want? Well, you can't wish us away. I've got eighteen years of my life invested in you. You ought to have stayed upstairs in my bed where you belong.

TROY: Rose . . . now listen to me . . . we can get a handle on this thing. We can talk this out . . . come to an understanding.

ROSE: All of a sudden it's "we." Where was "we" at when you was down there rolling around with some godforsaken woman? "We" should have come to an understanding before you started making a damn fool of yourself. You're a day late and a dollar short when it comes to an understanding with me.

TROY: It's just . . . She gives me a different idea . . . a different understanding about myself. I can step out of this

house and get away from the pressures and problems
. . . be a different man. I ain't got to wonder how I'm
gonna pay the bills or get the roof fixed. I can just be a
part of myself that I ain't never been.

ROSE: What I want to know . . . is do you plan to con-
tinue seeing her. That's all you can say to me.

TROY: I can sit up in her house and laugh. Do you understand what I'm saying. I can laugh out loud . . . and it
feels good. It reaches all the way down to the bottom of
my shoes.
(*Pause.*)
Rose, I can't give that up.

ROSE: Maybe you ought to go on and stay down there
with her . . . if she a better woman than me.

TROY: It ain't about nobody being a better woman or
nothing. Rose, you ain't the blame. A man couldn't ask
for no woman to be a better wife than you've been. I'm
responsible for it. I done locked myself into a pattern
trying to take care of you all that I forgot about myself.

ROSE: What the hell was I there for? That was my job, not
somebody else's.

TROY: Rose, I done tried all my life to live decent . . . to
live a clean . . . hard . . . useful life. I tried to be a good
husband to you. In every way I knew how. Maybe I
come into the world backwards, I don't know. But . . .
you born with two strikes on you before you come to the
plate. You got to guard it closely . . . always looking for
the curve-ball on the inside corner. You can't afford to
let none get past you. You can't afford a call strike. If
you going down . . . you going down swinging. Everything lined up against you. What you gonna do. I fooled
them, Rose. I bunted. When I found you and Cory and a

halfway decent job . . . I was safe. Couldn't nothing touch me. I wasn't gonna strike out no more. I wasn't going back to the penitentiary. I wasn't gonna lay in the streets with a bottle of wine. I was safe. I had me a family. A job. I wasn't gonna get that last strike. I was on first looking for one of them boys to knock me in. To get me home.

ROSE: You should have stayed in my bed, Troy.

TROY: Then when I saw that gal . . . she firmed up my backbone. And I got to thinking that if I tried . . . I just might be able to steal second. Do you understand after eighteen years I wanted to steal second.

ROSE: You should have held me tight. You should have grabbed me and held on.

TROY: I stood on first base for eighteen years and I thought . . . well, goddamn it . . . go on for it!

ROSE: We're not talking about baseball! We're talking about you going off to lay in bed with another woman . . . and then bring it home to me. That's what we're talking about. We ain't talking about no baseball.

TROY: Rose, you're not listening to me. I'm trying the best I can to explain it to you. It's not easy for me to admit that I been standing in the same place for eighteen years.

ROSE: I been standing with you! I been right here with you, Troy. I got a life too. I gave eighteen years of my life to stand in the same spot with you. Don't you think I ever wanted other things? Don't you think I had dreams and hopes? What about my life? What about me. Don't you think it ever crossed my mind to want to know other men? That I wanted to lay up somewhere and forget about my responsibilities? That I wanted someone to make me laugh so I could feel good? You not the only one who's got wants and needs. But I held on to you, Troy. I took all my feelings, my wants and needs, my dreams . . . and I buried them inside you. I planted a seed and watched and prayed over it. I planted myself inside you and waited to bloom. And it didn't take me no eighteen years to find out the soil was hard and rocky and it wasn't never gonna bloom.

But I held on to you, Troy. I held you tighter. You was my husband. I owed you everything I had. Every part of me I could find to give you. And upstairs in that room . . . with the darkness falling in on me . . . I gave everything I had to try and erase the doubt that you wasn't the finest man in the world. And wherever you was going . . . I wanted to be there with you. Cause you was my husband. Cause that's the only way I was gonna survive as your wife. You always talking about what you give . . . and what you don't have to give. But you take too. You take . . . and don't even know nobody's giving!

(*ROSE turns to exit into the house; TROY grabs her arm.*)

TROY: You say I take and don't give!

ROSE: Troy! You're hurting me!

TROY: You say I take and don't give.

ROSE: Troy . . . you're hurting my arm! Let go!

TROY: I done give you everything I got. Don't you tell that lie on me.

ROSE: Troy!

TROY: Don't you tell that lie on me!

(*CORY enters from the house.*)

CORY: Mama!

ROSE: Troy. You're hurting me.

TROY: Don't you tell me about no taking and giving.

(*CORY comes up behind TROY and grabs him. TROY, surprised, is thrown off balance just as CORY throws a glancing blow that catches him on the chest and knocks him down. TROY is stunned, as is CORY.*)

ROSE: Troy. Troy. No!
(*TROY gets to his feet and starts at CORY.*)
Troy . . . no. Please! Troy!
(*ROSE pulls on TROY to hold him back. TROY stops himself.*)

TROY: (*To CORY.*) Alright. That's strike two. You stay away from around me, boy. Don't you strike out. You living with a full count. Don't you strike out.
(*TROY exits out the yard as the lights go down.*)

It is six months later, early afternoon. TROY enters from the house and starts to exit the yard. ROSE enters from the house.

ROSE: Troy, I want to talk to you.

TROY: All of a sudden, after all this time, you want to talk to me, huh? You ain't wanted to talk to me for months. You ain't wanted to talk to me last night. You ain't wanted no part of me then. What you wanna talk to me about now?

ROSE: Tomorrow's Friday.

TROY: I know what day tomorrow is. You think I don't know tomorrow's Friday? My whole life I ain't done nothing but look to see Friday coming and you got to tell me it's Friday.

ROSE: I want to know if you're coming home.

TROY: I always come home, Rose. You know that. There ain't never been a night I ain't come home.

ROSE: That ain't what I mean . . . and you know it. I want to know if you're coming straight home after work.

TROY: I figure I'd cash my check . . . hang out at Taylors' with the boys . . . maybe play a game of checkers . . .

ROSE: Troy, I can't live like this. I won't live like this. You livin' on borrowed time with me. It's been going on six months now you ain't been coming home.

TROY: I be here every night. Every night of the year. That's 365 days.

ROSE: I want you to come home tomorrow after work.

TROY: Rose . . . I don't mess up my pay. You know that now. I take my pay and I give it to you. I don't have no money but what you give me back. I just want to have a little time to myself . . . a little time to enjoy life.

ROSE: What about me? When's my time to enjoy life?

TROY: I don't know what to tell you, Rose. I'm doing the best I can.

ROSE: You ain't been home from work but time enough to change your clothes and run out . . . and you wanna call that the best you can do?

TROY: I'm going over to the hospital to see Alberta. She went into the hospital this afternoon. Look like she might have the baby early. I won't be gone long.

ROSE: Well, you ought to know. They went over to Miss Pearl's and got Gabe today. She said you told them to go ahead and lock him up.

TROY: I ain't said no such thing. Whoever told you that is telling a lie. Pearl ain't doing nothing but telling a big fat lie.

ROSE: She ain't had to tell me. I read it on the papers.

TROY: I ain't told them nothing of the kind.

ROSE: I saw it right there on the papers.

TROY: What it say, huh?

ROSE: It said you told them to take him.

TROY: Then they screwed that up, just the way they screw up everything. I ain't worried about what they got on the paper.

ROSE: Say the government send part of his check to the hospital and the other part to you.

TROY: I ain't got nothing to do with that if that's the way it works. I ain't made up the rules about how it work.

ROSE: You did Gabe just like you did Cory. You wouldn't sign the paper for Cory . . . but you signed for Gabe. You signed that paper.

(*The telephone is heard ringing inside the house.*)

TROY: I told you I ain't signed nothing, woman! The only thing I signed was the release form. Hell, I can't read, I don't know what they had on that paper! I ain't signed nothing about sending Gabe away.

ROSE: I said send him to the hospital . . . you said let him be free . . . now you done went down there and signed him to the hospital for half his money. You went back on yourself, Troy. You gonna have to answer for that.

TROY: See now . . . you been over there talking to Miss Pearl. She done got mad cause she ain't getting Gabe's rent money. That's all it is. She's liable to say anything.

ROSE: Troy, I seen where you signed the paper.

TROY: You ain't seen nothing I signed. What she doing got papers on my brother anyway? Miss Pearl telling a big fat lie. And I'm gonna tell her about it too! You ain't

seen nothing I signed. Say . . . you ain't seen nothing I signed.
(*ROSE exits into the house to answer the telephone. Presently she returns*).

ROSE: Troy . . . that was the hospital. Alberta had the baby.

TROY: What she have? What is it?

ROSE: It's a girl.

TROY: I better get on down to the hospital to see her.

ROSE: Troy . . .

TROY: Rose . . . I got to go see her now. That's only right . . . what's the matter . . . the baby's alright, ain't it?

ROSE: Alberta died having the baby.

TROY: Died . . . you say she's dead? Alberta's dead?

ROSE: They said they done all they could. They couldn't do nothing for her.

TROY: The baby? How's the baby?

ROSE: They say it's healthy. I wonder who's gonna bury her.

TROY: She had family, Rose. She wasn't living in the world by herself.

ROSE: I know she wasn't living in the world by herself.

TROY: Next thing you gonna want to know if she had any insurance.

ROSE: Troy, you ain't got to talk like that.

TROY: That's the first thing that jumped out your mouth.

"Who's gonna bury her?" Like I'm fixing to take on that task for myself.

ROSE: I am your wife. Don't push me away.

TROY: I ain't pushing nobody away. Just give me some space. That's all. Just give me some room to breathe.

(*ROSE exits into the house. TROY walks about the yard.*)

TROY: (*With a quiet rage that threatens to consume him.*) Alright . . . Mr. Death. See now . . . I'm gonna tell you what I'm gonna do. I'm gonna take and build me a fence around this yard. See? I'm gonna build me a fence around what belongs to me. And then I want you to stay on the other side. See? You stay over there until you're ready for me. Then you come on. Bring your army. Bring your sickle. Bring your wrestling clothes. I ain't gonna fall down on my vigilance this time. You ain't gonna sneak up on me no more. When you ready for me . . . when the top of your list say Troy Maxson . . . that's when you come around here. You come up and knock on the front door. Ain't nobody else got nothing to do with this. This is between you and me. Man to man. You stay on the other side of that fence until you ready for me. Then you come up and knock on the front door. Anytime you want. I'll be ready for you.
(*The lights go down to black.*)

Act Two

The lights come up on the porch. It is late evening three days later. ROSE sits listening to the ball game waiting for TROY. The final out of the game is made and ROSE switches off the radio. TROY enters the yard carrying an infant wrapped in blankets. He stands back from the house and calls.

(*ROSE enters and stands on the porch. There is a long, awkward silence, the weight of which grows heavier with each passing second.*)

TROY: Rose . . . I'm standing here with my daughter in my arms. She ain't but a wee bittie little old thing. She don't know nothing about grownups' business. She innocent . . . and she ain't got no mama.

ROSE: What you telling me for, Troy?
(*She turns and exits into the house.*)

TROY: Well . . . I guess we'll just sit out here on the porch.
(*He sits down on the porch. There is an awkward indelicateness about the way he handles the baby. His large-*

ness engulfs and seems to swallow it. He speaks loud enough for ROSE *to hear.*)

A man's got to do what's right for him. I ain't sorry for nothing I done. It felt right in my heart.

(*To the baby.*)

What you smiling at? Your daddy's a big man. Got these great big old hands. But sometimes he's scared. And right now your daddy's scared cause we sitting out here and ain't got no home. Oh, I been homeless before. I ain't had no little baby with me. But I been homeless. You just be out on the road by your lonesome and you see one of them trains coming and you just kinda go like this . . .

(*He sings as a lullaby.*)

Please, Mr. Engineer let a man ride the line
Please, Mr. Engineer let a man ride the line
I ain't got no ticket please let me ride the blinds

(ROSE *enters from the house.* TROY *hearing her steps behind him, stands and faces her.*)

She's my daughter, Rose. My own flesh and blood. I can't deny her no more than I can deny them boys.

(*Pause.*)

You and them boys is my family. You and them and this child is all I got in the world. So I guess what I'm saying is . . . I'd appreciate it if you'd help me take care of her.

ROSE: Okay, Troy . . . you're right. I'll take care of your baby for you . . . cause . . . like you say . . . she's innocent . . . and you can't visit the sins of the father upon the child. A motherless child has got a hard time.

(*She takes the baby from him.*)

From right now . . . this child got a mother. But you a womanless man.

(ROSE *turns and exits into the house with the baby. Lights go down to black.*)

Act Two

It is two months later. LYONS enters from the street. He knocks on the door and calls

LYONS: Hey, Rose! (*Pause.*) Rose!

ROSE: (*From inside the house.*) Stop that yelling. You gonna wake up Raynell. I just got her to sleep.

LYONS: I just stopped by to pay Papa this twenty dollars I owe him. Where's Papa at?

ROSE: He should be here in a minute. I'm getting ready to go down to the church. Sit down and wait on him.

LYONS: I got to go pick up Bonnie over her mother's house.

ROSE: Well, sit it down there on the table. He'll get it.

LYONS: (*Enters the house and sets the money on the table.*) Tell Papa I said thanks. I'll see you again.

ROSE: Alright, Lyons. We'll see you.

(*LYONS starts to exit as CORY enters*)

CORY: Hey, Lyons.

LYONS: What's happening, Cory. Say man, I'm sorry I missed your graduation. You know I had a gig and couldn't get away. Otherwise, I would have been there, man. So what you doing?

CORY: I'm trying to find a job.

LYONS: Yeah I know how that go, man. It's rough out here. Jobs are scarce.

CORY: Yeah, I know.

LYONS: Look here, I got to run. Talk to Papa . . . he know some people. He'll be able to help get you a job. Talk to him . . . see what he say.

CORY: Yeah . . . alright, Lyons.

LYONS: You take care. I'll talk to you soon. We'll find some time to talk.

(*LYONS exits the yard. CORY wanders over to the tree, picks up the bat and assumes a batting stance. He studies an imaginary pitcher and swings. Dissatisfied with the result, he tries again. TROY enters. They eye each other for a beat. CORY puts the bat down and exits the yard. TROY starts into the house as ROSE exits with RAYNELL. She is carrying a cake.*)

TROY: I'm coming in and everybody's going out.

ROSE: I'm taking this cake down to the church for the bakesale. Lyons was by to see you. He stopped by to pay you your twenty dollars. It's laying in there on the table.

TROY: (*Going into his pocket.*) Well . . . here go this money.

ROSE: Put it in there on the table, Troy. I'll get it.

TROY: What time you coming back?

ROSE: Ain't no use in you studying me. It don't matter what time I come back.

TROY: I just asked you a question, woman. What's the matter . . . can't I ask you a question?

ROSE: Troy, I don't want to go into it. Your dinner's in there on the stove. All you got to do is heat it up. And don't you be eating the rest of them cakes in there. I'm coming back for them. We having a bakesale at the church tomorrow.

(*ROSE exits the yard. TROY sits down on the steps, takes a pint bottle from his pocket, opens it and drinks. He begins to sing.*)

TROY:
Hear it ring! Hear it ring!
Had an old dog his name was Blue
You know Blue was mighty true
You know Blue as a good old dog
Blue trees a possum in a hollow log
You know from that he was a good old dog

(*BONO enters the yard.*)

BONO: Hey, Troy.

TROY: Hey, what's happening, Bono?

BONO: I just thought I'd stop by to see you.

TROY: What you stop by and see me for? You ain't stopped by in a month of Sundays. Hell, I must owe you money or something.

BONO· Since you got your promotion I can't keep up with you. Used to see you everyday. Now I don't even know what route you working.

TROY: They keep switching me around. Got me out in Greentree now . . . hauling white folks' garbage.

BONO: Greentree, huh? You lucky, at least you ain't got to be lifting them barrels. Damn if they ain't getting heavier. I'm gonna put in my two years and call it quits.

TROY: I'm thinking about retiring myself.

BONO: You got it easy. You can *drive* for another five years.

TROY: It ain't the same, Bono. It ain't like working the back of the truck. Ain't got nobody to talk to . . . feel like you working by yourself. Naw, I'm thinking about retiring. How's Lucille?

BONO: She alright. Her arthritis get to acting up on her sometime. Saw Rose on my way in. She going down to the church, huh?

TROY: Yeah, she took up going down there. All them preachers looking for somebody to fatten their pockets.
(*Pause.*)
Got some gin here.

BONO: Naw, thanks. I just stopped by to say hello.

TROY: Hell, nigger . . . you can take a drink. I ain't never known you to say no to a drink. You ain't got to work tomorrow.

BONO: I just stopped by. I'm fixing to go over to Skinner's. We got us a domino game going over his house every Friday.

TROY: Nigger, you can't play no dominoes. I used to whup you four games out of five.

BONO: Well, that learned me. I'm getting better.

TROY: Yeah? Well, that's alright.

BONO: Look here . . . I got to be getting on. Stop by sometime, huh?

TROY: Yeah, I'll do that, Bono. Lucille told Rose you bought her a new refrigerator.

BONO: Yeah, Rose told Lucille you had finally built your fence . . . so I figured we'd call it even.

TROY: I knew you would.

BONO: Yeah . . . okay. I'll be talking to you.

TROY: Yeah, take care, Bono. Good to see you. I'm gonna stop over.

BONO: Yeah. Okay, Troy.
(*BONO exits. TROY drinks from the bottle.*)

TROY:
Old Blue died and I dig his grave
Let him down with a golden chain
Every night when I hear old Blue bark
I know Blue treed a possum in Noah's Ark.
Hear it ring! Hear it ring!

(*CORY enters the yard. They eye each other for a beat. TROY is sitting in the middle of the steps. CORY walks over.*)

CORY: I got to get by.

TROY: Say what? What's you say?

CORY: You in my way. I got to get by.

TROY: You got to get by where? This is my house. Bought and paid for. In full. Took me fifteen years. And if you wanna go in my house and I'm sitting on the steps . . . you say excuse me. Like your mama taught you.

CORY: Come on, Pop . . . I got to get by.

(*CORY starts to maneuver his way past* TROY. TROY *grabs his leg and shoves him back.*)

TROY: You just gonna walk over top of me?

CORY: I live here too!

TROY: (*Advancing toward him.*) You just gonna walk over top of me in my own house?

CORY: I ain't scared of you.

TROY: I ain't asked if you was scared of me. I asked you if you was fixing to walk over top of me in my own house? That's the question. You ain't gonna say excuse me? You just gonna walk over top of me?

CORY: If you wanna put it like that.

TROY: How else am I gonna put it?

CORY: I was walking by you to go into the house cause you sitting on the steps drunk, singing to yourself. You can put it like that.

TROY: Without saying excuse me???
(*CORY doesn't respond.*)
I asked you a question. Without saying excuse me???

CORY: I ain't got to say excuse me to you. You don't count around here no more.

TROY: Oh, I see . . . I don't count around here no more. You ain't got to say excuse me to your daddy. All of a sudden you done got so grown that your daddy don't count around here no more . . . Around here in his own house and yard that he done paid for with the sweat of his brow. You done got so grown to where you gonna take over. You gonna take over my house. Is that right?

You gonna wear my pants. You gonna go in there and stretch out on my bed. You ain't got to say excuse me cause I don't count around here no more. Is that right?

CORY: That's right. You always talking this dumb stuff. Now, why don't you just get out my way.

TROY: I guess you got someplace to sleep and something to put in your belly. You got that, huh? You got that? That's what you need. You got that, huh?

CORY: You don't know what I got. You ain't got to worry about what I got.

TROY: You right! You one hundred percent right! I done spent the last seventeen years worrying about what you got. Now it's your turn, see? I'll tell you what to do. You grown . . . we done established that. You a man. Now, let's see you act like one. Turn your behind around and walk out this yard. And when you get out there in the alley . . . you can forget about this house. See? Cause this is my house. You go on and be a man and get your own house. You can forget about this. 'Cause this is mine. You go on and get yours cause I'm through with doing for you.

CORY: You talking about what you did for me . . . what'd you ever give me?

TROY: Them feet and bones! That pumping heart, nigger! I give you more than anybody else is ever gonna give you.

CORY: You ain't never gave me nothing! You ain't never done nothing but hold me back. Afraid I was gonna be better than you. All you ever did was try and make me scared of you. I used to tremble every time you called my name. Every time I heard your footsteps in the house. Wondering all the time . . . what's Papa gonna say if I do this? . . . What's he gonna say if I do that? . . . What's Papa gonna say if I turn on the radio? And Mama, too . . . she tries . . . but she's scared of you.

TROY: You leave your mama out of this. She ain't got nothing to do with this.

CORY: I don't know how she stand you . . . after what you did to her.

TROY: I told you to leave your mama out of this!
(*He advances toward CORY.*)

CORY: What you gonna do . . . give me a whupping? You can't whup me no more. You're too old. You just an old man.

TROY: (*Shoves him on his shoulder.*) Nigger! That's what you are. You just another nigger on the street to me!

CORY: You crazy! You know that?

TROY: Go on now! You got the devil in you. Get on away from me!

CORY: You just a crazy old man . . . talking about I got the devil in me.

TROY: Yeah, I'm crazy! If you don't get on the other side of that yard . . . I'm gonna show you how crazy I am! Go on . . . get the hell out of my yard.

CORY: It ain't your yard. You took Uncle Gabe's money he got from the army to buy this house and then you put him out.

TROY: (*TROY advances on CORY.*) Get your black ass out of my yard!

(*TROY's advance backs CORY up against the tree. CORY grabs up the bat.*)

CORY: I ain't going nowhere! Come on . . . put me out! I ain't scared of you.

TROY: That's my bat!

CORY: Come on!

TROY: Put my bat down!

CORY: Come on, put me out.
(*CORY swings at* TROY, *who backs across the yard.*)
What's the matter? You so bad . . . put me out!

(*TROY advances toward* CORY.)

CORY: (*Backing up.*) Come on! Come on!

TROY: You're gonna have to use it! You wanna draw that bat back on me . . . you're gonna have to use it.

CORY: Come on! . . . Come on!

(*CORY swings the bat at* TROY *a second time. He misses.* TROY *continues to advance toward him.*)

TROY: You're gonna have to kill me! You wanna draw that bat back on me. You're gonna have to kill me.

(*CORY, backed up against the tree, can go no farther.* TROY *taunts him. He sticks out his head and offers him a target.*)

Come on! Come on!

(*CORY is unable to swing the bat.* TROY *grabs it.*)

TROY: Then I'll show you.

(*CORY and* TROY *struggle over the bat. The struggle is fierce and fully engaged.* TROY *ultimately is the stronger, and takes the bat from* CORY *and stands over him ready to swing. He stops himself.*)

Go on and get away from around my house.

(*CORY, stung by his defeat, picks himself up, walks slowly out of the yard and up the alley.*)

CORY: Tell Mama I'll be back for my things.

TROY: They'll be on the other side of that fence.

(*CORY exits.*)

TROY: I can't taste nothing. Helluljah! I can't taste nothing no more. (*TROY assumes a batting posture and begins to taunt Death, the fastball in the outside corner.*) Come on! It's between you and me now! Come on! Anytime you want! Come on! I be ready for you . . . but I ain't gonna be easy.

(*The lights go down on the scene.*)

Act Two

The time is 1965. The lights come up in the yard. It is the morning of TROY's *funeral. A funeral plaque with a light hangs beside the door. There is a small garden plot off to the side. There is noise and activity in the house as* ROSE, GABRIEL *and* BONO *have gathered. The door opens and* RAYNELL, *seven years old, enters dressed in a flannel nightgown. She crosses to the garden and pokes around with a stick.* ROSE *calls from the house.*

ROSE: Raynell!

RAYNELL: Mam?

ROSE: What you doing out there?

RAYNELL: Nothing.

*(*ROSE *comes to the door.)*

ROSE: Girl, get in here and get dressed. What you doing?

RAYNELL: Seeing if my garden growed.

ROSE: I told you it ain't gonna grow overnight. You got to wait.

RAYNELL: It don't look like it never gonna grow. Dag!

ROSE: I told you a watched pot never boils. Get in here and get dressed.

RAYNELL: This ain't even no pot, Mama.

ROSE: You just have to give it a chance. It'll grow. Now you come on and do what I told you. We got to be getting ready. This ain't no morning to be playing around. You hear me?

RAYNELL: Yes, mam.

(ROSE *exits into the house.* RAYNELL *continues to poke at her garden with a stick.* CORY *enters. He is dressed in a Marine corporal's uniform, and carries a duffel bag. His posture is that of a military man, and his speech has a clipped sternness.*)

CORY: (*To* RAYNELL.) Hi.
(*Pause.*)
I bet your name is Raynell.

RAYNELL: Uh huh.

CORY: Is your mama home?

(RAYNELL *runs up on the porch and calls through the screendoor.*)

RAYNELL: Mama . . . there's some man out here. Mama?

(ROSE *comes to the door.*)

ROSE: Cory? Lord have mercy! Look here, you all!
(ROSE *and* CORY *embrace in a tearful reunion as* BONO *and* LYONS *enter from the house dressed in funeral clothes.*)

BONO: Aw, looka here . . .

ROSE: Done got all grown up!

CORY: Don't cry, Mama. What you crying about?

ROSE: I'm just so glad you made it.

CORY: Hey Lyons. How you doing, Mr. Bono.

(*LYONS goes to embrace CORY.*)

LYONS: Look at you, man. Look at you. Don't he look good, Rose. Got them Corporal stripes.

ROSE: What took you so long.

CORY: You know how the Marines are, Mama. They got to get all their paperwork straight before they let you do anything.

ROSE: Well, I'm sure glad you made it. They let Lyons come. Your Uncle Gabe's still in the hospital. They don't know if they gonna let him out or not. I just talked to them a little while ago.

LYONS: A Corporal in the United States Marines.

BONO: Your daddy knew you had it in you. He used to tell me all the time.

LYONS: Don't he look good, Mr. Bono?

BONO: Yeah, he remind me of Troy when I first met him. (*Pause.*)
Say, Rose, Lucille's down at the church with the choir. I'm gonna go down and get the pallbearers lined up. I'll be back to get you all.

ROSE: Thanks, Jim.

CORY: See you, Mr. Bono.

LYONS: (*With his arm around RAYNELL.*) Cory . . . look at Raynell. Ain't she precious? She gonna break a whole lot of hearts.

ROSE: Raynell, come and say hello to your brother. This is your brother, Cory. You remember Cory.

RAYNELL: No, Mam.

CORY: She don't remember me, Mama.

ROSE: Well, we talk about you. She heard us talk about you.
(*To RAYNELL.*) This is your brother, Cory. Come on and say hello.

RAYNELL: Hi.

CORY: Hi. So you're Raynell. Mama told me a lot about you.

ROSE: You all come on into the house and let me fix you some breakfast. Keep up your strength.

CORY: I ain't hungry, Mama.

LYONS: You can fix me something, Rose. I'll be in there in a minute.

ROSE: Cory, you sure you don't want nothing. I know they ain't feeding you right.

CORY: No, Mama . . . thanks. I don't feel like eating. I'll get something later.

ROSE: Raynell . . . get on upstairs and get that dress on like I told you.

(*ROSE and RAYNELL exit into the house.*)

LYONS: So . . . I hear you thinking about getting married.

CORY: Yeah, I done found the right one, Lyons. It's about time.

LYONS: Me and Bonnie been split up about four years now. About the time Papa retired. I guess she just got

tired of all them changes I was putting her through.
(*Pause.*)
I always knew you was gonna make something out yourself. Your head was always in the right direction. So . . .
you gonna stay in . . . make it a career . . . put in your
twenty years?

CORY: I don't know. I got six already, I think that's
enough.

LYONS: Stick with Uncle Sam and retire early. Ain't nothing out here. I guess Rose told you what happened with
me. They got me down the workhouse. I thought I was
being slick cashing other people's checks.

CORY: How much time you doing?

LYONS: They give me three years. I got that beat now. I
ain't got but nine more months. It ain't so bad. You learn
to deal with it like anything else. You got to take the
crookeds with the straights. That's what Papa used to
say. He used to say that when he struck out. I seen him
strike out three times in a row . . . and the next time up
he hit the ball over the grandstand. Right out there in
Homestead Field. He wasn't satisfied hitting in the seats
. . . he want to hit it over everything! After the game he
had two hundred people standing around waiting to
shake his hand. You got to take the crookeds with the
straights. Yeah, Papa was something else.

CORY: You still playing?

LYONS: Cory . . . you know I'm gonna do that. There's
some fellows down there we got us a band . . . we gonna
try and stay together when we get out . . . but yeah, I'm
still playing. It still nelps me to get out of bed in the
morning. As long as it do that I'm gonna be right there
playing and trying to make some sense out of it.

ROSE: (*Calling.*) Lyons, I got these eggs in the pan.

LYONS: Let me go on and get these eggs, man. Get ready
to go bury Papa.
(*Pause.*)
How you doing? You doing alright?

(*CORY nods. LYONS touches him on the shoulder and
they share a moment of silent grief. LYONS exits into
the house. CORY wanders about the yard. RAYNELL
enters.*)

RAYNELL: Hi.

CORY: Hi.

RAYNELL: Did you used to sleep in my room?

CORY: Yeah . . . that used to be my room.

RAYNELL: That's what Papa call it. "Cory's room." It got
your football in the closet.

(*ROSE comes to the door.*)

ROSE: Raynell, get in there and get them good shoes on.

RAYNELL: Mama, can't I wear these. Them other one hurt
my feet.

ROSE: Well, they just gonna have to hurt your feet for a
while. You ain't said they hurt your feet when you went
down to the store and got them.

RAYNELL: They didn't hurt then. My feet done got bigger.

ROSE: Don't you give me no backtalk now. You get in
there and get them shoes on.
(*RAYNELL exits into the house.*)
Ain't too much changed. He still got that piece of rag tied
to that tree. He was out here swinging that bat. I was just
ready to go back in the house. He swung that bat and

bat and then he just fell over. Seem like he swung it and stood there with this grin on his face . . . and then he just fell over. They carried him on down to the hospital, but I knew there wasn't no need . . . why don't you come on in the house?

CORY: Mama . . . I got something to tell you. I don't know how to tell you this . . . but I've got to tell you . . . I'm not going to Papa's funeral.

ROSE: Boy, hush your mouth. That's your daddy you talking about. I don't want hear that kind of talk this morning. I done raised you to come to this? You standing there all healthy and grown talking about you ain't going to your daddy's funeral?

CORY: Mama . . . listen . . .

ROSE: I don't want to hear it, Cory. You just get that thought out of your head.

CORY: I can't drag Papa with me everywhere I go. I've got to say no to him. One time in my life I've got to say no.

ROSE: Don't nobody have to listen to nothing like that. I know you and your daddy ain't seen eye to eye, but I ain't got to listen to that kind of talk this morning. Whatever was between you and your daddy . . . the time has come to put it aside. Just take it and set it over there on the shelf and forget about it. Disrespecting your daddy ain't gonna make you a man, Cory. You got to find a way to come to that on your own. Not going to your daddy's funeral ain't gonna make you a man.

CORY: The whole time I was growing up . . . living in his house . . . Papa was like a shadow that followed you everywhere. It weighed on you and sunk into your flesh.

It would wrap around you and lay there until you couldn't tell which one was you anymore. That shadow digging in your flesh. Trying to crawl in. Trying to live through you. Everywhere I looked, Troy Maxson was staring back at me . . . hiding under the bed . . . in the closet. I'm just saying I've got to find a way to get rid of that shadow, Mama.

ROSE: You just like him. You got him in you good.

CORY: Don't tell me that, Mama.

ROSE: You Troy Maxson all over again.

CORY: I don't want to be Troy Maxson. I want to be me.

ROSE: You can't be nobody but who you are, Cory. That shadow wasn't nothing but you growing into yourself. You either got to grow into it or cut it down to fit you. But that's all you got to make life with. That's all you got to measure yourself against that world out there. Your daddy wanted you to be everything he wasn't . . . and at the same time he tried to make you into everything he was. I don't know if he was right or wrong . . . but I do know he meant to do more good than he meant to do harm. He wasn't always right. Sometimes when he touched he bruised. And sometimes when he took me in his arms he cut.
When I first met your daddy I thought . . . Here is a man I can lay down with and make a baby. That's the first thing I thought when I seen him. I was thirty years old and had done seen my share of men. But when he walked up to me and said, "I can dance a waltz that'll make you dizzy," I thought, Rose Lee, here is a man that you can open yourself up to and be filled to bursting. Here is a man that can fill all them empty spaces you been tipping around the edges of. One of them empty spaces was being somebody's mother.

I married your daddy and settled down to cooking his supper and keeping clean sheets on the bed. When your daddy walked through the house he was so big he filled it up. That was my first mistake. Not to make him leave some room for me. For my part in the matter. But at that time I wanted that. I wanted a house that I could sing in. And that's what your daddy gave me. I didn't know to keep up his strength I had to give up little pieces of mine. I did that. I took on his life as mine and mixed up the pieces so that you couldn't hardly tell which was which anymore. It was my choice. It was my life and I didn't have to live it like that. But that's what life offered me in the way of being a woman and I took it. I grabbed hold of it with both hands.

By the time Raynell came into the house, me and your daddy had done lost touch with one another. I didn't want to make my blessing off of nobody's misfortune . . but I took on to Raynell like she was all them babies I had wanted and never had.

(*The phone rings.*)

Like I'd been blessed to relive a part of my life. And if the Lord see fit to keep up my strength . . . I'm gonna do her just like your daddy did you . . . I'm gonna give her the best of what's in me.

RAYNELL: (*Entering, still with her old shoes.*) Mama . . . Reverend Tollivier on the phone.

(*ROSE exits into the house.*)

RAYNELL: Hi.

CORY: Hi.

RAYNELL: You in the Army or the Marines?

CORY: Marines.

RAYNELL: Papa said it was the Army. Did you know Blue?

CORY: Blue? Who's Blue?

RAYNELL: Papa's dog what he sing about all the time.

CORY: (*Singing*.) Hear it ring! Hear it ring!
I had a dog his name was Blue
You know Blue was mighty true
You know Blue was a good old dog
Blue treed a possum in a hollow log
You know from that he was a good old dog.
Hear it ring! Hear it ring!

(RAYNELL *joins in singing*.)

CORY and RAYNELL: Blue treed a possum out on a limb
Blue looked at me and I looked at him
Grabbed that possum and put him in a sack
Blue stayed there till I came back
Old Blue's feets was big and round
Never allowed a possum to touch the ground.

Old Blue died and I dug his grave
I dug his grave with a silver spade
Let him down with a golden chain
And every night I call his name
Go on Blue, you good dog you
Go on Blue, you good dog you

RAYNELL: Blue laid down and died like a man
Blue laid down and died . . .

BOTH: Blue laid down and died like a man
Now he's treeing possums in the Promised Land
I'm gonna tell you this to let you know
Blue's gone where the good dogs go
When I hear old Blue bark

When I hear old Blue bark
Blue treed a possum in Noah's Ark
Blue treed a possum in Noah's Ark.

(*ROSE comes to the screen door.*)

ROSE: Cory, we gonna be ready to go in a minute.

CORY: (*To RAYNELL.*) You go on in the house and change them shoes like Mama told you so we can go to Papa's funeral.

RAYNELL: Okay, I'll be back.

(*RAYNELL exits into the house. CORY gets up and crosses over to the tree. ROSE stands in the screen door watching him. GABRIEL enters from the alley.*)

GABRIEL: (*Calling.*) Hey, Rose!

ROSE: Gabe?

GABRIEL: I'm here, Rose. Hey Rose, I'm here!

(*ROSE enters from the house.*)

ROSE: Lord . . . Look here, Lyons!

LYONS: See, I told you, Rose . . . I told you they'd let him come.

CORY: How you doing, Uncle Gabe?

LYONS: How you doing, Uncle Gabe?

GABRIEL: Hey, Rose. It's time. It's time to tell St. Peter to open the gates. Troy, you ready? You ready, Troy. I'm gonna tell St. Peter to open the gates. You get ready now.
(*Gabriel, with great fanfare, braces himself to blow. The trumpet is without a mouthpiece. He puts the end of it into his mouth and blows with great force, like a man*)

who has been waiting some twenty-odd years for this single moment. No sound comes out of the trumpet. He braces himself and blows again with the same result. A third time he blows. There is a weight of impossible description that falls away and leaves him bare and exposed to a frightful realization. It is a trauma that a sane and normal mind would be unable to withstand. He begins to dance. A slow, strange dance, eerie and life-giving. A dance of atavistic signature and ritual. LYONS attempts to embrace him. GABRIEL pushes LYONS away. He begins to howl in what is an attempt at song, or perhaps a song turning back into itself in an attempt at speech. He finishes his dance and the gates of heaven stand open as wide as God's closet.)
That's the way that go!

(BLACKOUT.)

August Wilson

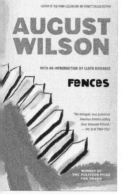

978-0-452-26401-4

978-0-452-26534-9

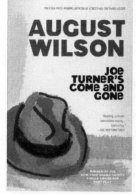

978-0-452-26009-2

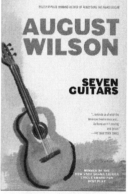

978-0-452-27692-5

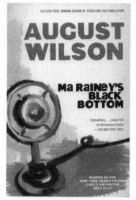

978-0-452-26113-6

<u>Two Trains Running</u>
978-0-452-26929-3

Available wherever books are sold.

UME

imprint of Penguin Group (USA) Inc.
w.penguin.com